GW00504250

Breast Feeding –
How to Succeed

by the same author

FUNDAMENTALS OF OBSTETRICS AND GYNAECOLOGY
    Volume 1   Obstetrics
    Volume 2   Gynaecology

EVERYWOMAN

HUMAN REPRODUCTION AND SOCIETY

PEOPLE POPULATING

BREAST FEEDING —
How to Succeed

Questions and answers for mothers

Derek Llewellyn-Jones
OBE, MD, MAO, FRCOG, FRACOG

faber and faber

First published in 1983
by Faber and Faber Limited
3 Queen Square, London WC1N 3AU
Reprinted 1983
Filmset in Monophoto Times
Printed in England by
Fletcher & Son Ltd,
Norwich

British Library Cataloguing in Publication Data

Llewellyn-Jones Derek
Breast feeding
1. Breast feeding
I. Title
649'.3   RJ216

ISBN 0–571–13003–8
ISBN 0–571–13004–6 Pbk

Library of Congress Cataloging in Publication Data

Llewellyn-Jones, Derek
  Breast feeding, how to succeed

  Bibliography: p.
  Includes index.
  1. Breast feeding I. Title
RJ216.L66 1983   649'.3   82–21051
ISBN 0–571–13003–8
ISBN 0–571–13004–6 (pbk)

Contents

Illustrations

TABLES

Preface

In the past few years there has been a modest but significant return to breast feeding. The reasons for the change are not clear but the influence of women's organizations is evident. As more women choose to breast feed, there is a greater need for books which help women to understand how lactation occurs, how it is established and maintained and which answer the questions breast-feeding mothers ask. This book was written after discussions with members of the Nursing Mothers' Association of Australia who kindly conducted a survey of the questions their counsellors in New South Wales were asked most frequently over a six-month period. The draft manuscript was read and commented upon by members of the Association and I am particularly grateful to Rae Paterson who arranged this and to Gael Walker who provided me with the annotated reading list. I am grateful to Shirley Breese of the Childbirth and Parenting Association of Victoria who also read and commented on the manuscript. I have been fortunate, once again, that Audrey Besterman was able to convert my crude sketches into delightful illustrations. My secretary, Carole Kirkland, has patiently typed and re-typed the manuscript, so that a clean copy was sent to Patricia Downie, Medical and Nursing Editor, Faber and Faber Ltd, who edits my books with such skill.

Glossary

Atopy An inherited tendency to be extra sensitive to foreign proteins (allergens) either ingested or injected. It is a form of allergy.
In atopic families the father or the mother have, or have had, hay
fever, eczema or asthma.

Beta-lactoglobulin One of the milk proteins which make up the whey
of cow's milk. It is not found in human milk and may be a cause
of some cases of infantile eczema, colic and asthma.

Colostrum The milk-like substance secreted by the breasts in pregnancy and in the first three or four days after childbirth. It is
lemon yellow in colour, and contains anti-infective substances (see
p. 75).

DES Diethyl stilboestrol (DES) is a synthetic oestrogen hormone.
In the 1940s and 1950s DES was given to some pregnant women
to prevent them aborting. A number of the female children of
those mothers have developed a form of vaginal cancer which is
believed to be due to the effects of DES on the genital tract when
they were growing in their mothers' wombs.

'Doula' concept This concept was introduced by Dana Raphael who
describes the need for a breast-feeding mother to be mothered. A
doula is an informed, empathetic helper, who 'mothers' the mother
so that she is better able to adjust to parenthood and to establish
and maintain lactation. A doula helps the mother to obtain the
confidence that she can cope, that she is a competent mother and,
at the same time, a person in her own right. A doula also helps
the mother take time off from mothering knowing that her baby
will be cared for competently.

Foremilk The first portion of the milk 'let-down' and available to
the baby is the 'foremilk'.

Galactosaemia An inborn error of metabolism affecting one baby in every 50 000. The baby is unable to breakdown the milk sugar, galactose, into simpler sugars in its body with the result that galactose accumulates, leading to lethargy, jaundice and failure to gain weight. It is treated by discontinuing all milk and milk products.

Gestagen A synthetic form of progesterone (one of the female sex hormones made in the ovaries) which is used in the Pill, as a single contraceptive (the Mini-pill; the injectable) and to treat menstrual disorders. Also called progestogen and progestin.

HPL Human placental lactogen (HPL) is a substance secreted by the placenta during pregnancy. One of its functions is to prepare the milk-secreting cells of the breasts for the action of prolactin.

Hindmilk The milk 'let-down' in the later part of a breast feed is called hindmilk.

Immunoglobulins A group of proteins found in body fluids which are produced by specialized cells and act to protect the body from infections. They are also called antibodies.

kcal The term is short for kilocalories or Calories. The number of calories in food gives a measure of the energy intake, and the number of kcals used to perform bodily functions, including exercise gives a measure of energy expenditure. Recently after several conferences, it has been decided internationally that the measure of energy will in future be a joule (J). A kilojoule (kJ) equals 1000J, and 1kcal equals 4.19 kJ.

Keratomalacia A condition of the eye where there is dryness, and possibly ulceration of the cornea. It is caused by a severe deficiency of vitamin A.

Lactoferrin A protein found in milk which inhibits the growth of certain bacteria in the baby's intestines. It also binds with iron in the diet, and if the amount of iron is too high, there may be no 'free' lactoferrin to act on the bacteria.

Lysosyme An anti-infective protein which forms part of the whey of human milk (it is not found in cow's milk). Lysosymes act together with one of the immunoglobulins (IgA) to kill bacteria.

MJ An MJ is a megajoule, which is 1000 kilojoules. 1MJ = 239kcals.

Macrophages These are the large wandering 'killer' or scavenger cells found in the blood. They seek and destroy bacteria and other 'foreign' proteins.

Pap   The term given in the 18th century to the mixture of bread and water, or bread and cow's milk which was fed to an abandoned baby, or to a baby whose mother thought she had insufficient breast milk for him.

Phenylketonuria   Some proteins, including those in milk, contain a substance called phenylalanine. In the human body this is broken down by an enzyme to simpler substances. One baby in every 10 000 lacks the enzyme, which permits phenylalanine to accumulate in his body. Over a period this leads to irreversible mental retardation. Babies with the enzyme defect can be detected within seven days of birth by a special test on a drop of their blood. If the condition phenylketonuria is found, mental retardation can be prevented if the baby is given a special diet.

'Rooting' reflex   If the mother's nipple (or some other stimulus) touches the baby's cheek, he will turn his head from side to side searching for the nipple until his mouth finds it.

Sex hormones   These are the hormones produced by the ovaries in women (and the testes in men). In women the main sex hormones are oestrogen and progesterone but a small quantity of the male hormone, testosterone, is also produced.

PART ONE

Preparing for breast feeding

Breast feeding cannot occur unless the breasts are stimulated to lactate or to produce milk. A knowledge of the way the female breasts develop, of their anatomy and of the changes which occur during the menstrual cycle and pregnancy enables a woman to understand the rather complex way in which milk is made. This understanding will help her to become confident about her ability to breast feed. And successful breast feeding is a 'confidence trick'.

DEVELOPMENT OF THE BREAST

In humans, the breasts start to develop in the third month of fetal life, when solid tubes of cells grow inwards into the tissues over the chest from two depressions in the skin, one on each side of the midline. Early in the second half of pregnancy, the solid tubes of cells become hollow, forming ducts, and begin to divide into branches (Fig. 1). The depressions in the skin will eventually become the nipples and each of the ducts will end in one of them. At first the nipple is inverted, and this may persist until after the baby has been born. In most cases it then changes and protrudes above the skin to form a recognizable nipple. In a few babies, the nipple remains inverted and depressed below the skin, and this may persist until adulthood.

By the time the baby is born, each breast consists of a nipple to which between 10 and 20 ducts are connected. The growth and branching of the ducts which have occurred during the baby's life in the uterus are due to the effect of the sex hormones, oestrogen and progesterone, which are secreted by the placenta during pregnancy. Once the baby has been born, these hormones cease to stimulate the breasts, which will remain quiescent until puberty.

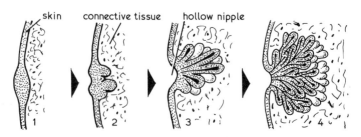

Fig. 1   How the breast develops. (1) A thickening appears in the skin;
(2) The thickening develops 'buds' which grow inwards; (3)
The buds become hollow; (4) The buds branch

At puberty, the flat breasts and small nipples which have made
the chests of boys and girls indistinguishable begin to change. A
girl's breasts begin to develop because of the female sex hormones
which are secreted by her ovaries. At first the area around the nipple
increases in size, so that a small swollen disc surrounds the nipple.
As the months pass, the breasts continue to increase in size until
they become protuberant and conical in shape (Fig. 2).

It may help to understand the changes which occur in the breast
during puberty and later during pregnancy if something of the anatomy of the breast is known.

The breast has been described, graphically, by Dr Applebaum of
Miami, Florida, as a 'forest consisting of ten or twenty trees all
intimately bound together by interweaving vines and vegetation.
Each tree is complete with its own root system and is covered by the
ground.' The milk trees are the 10 or 20 hollow ducts which grew
during fetal life into the underlying tissues from the depressed pit.
They are more correctly called 'lactiferous duct systems'. Each lactiferous duct system ends in the nipple, where the duct is often dilated
to form a tiny 'reservoir'. Each milk tree grows branches and twigs
or, more correctly, ducts and ductules, under the influence of the sex
hormones oestrogen and progesterone. At the end of the twigs
(ductules) multiple clusters of 'leaves' are formed. The leaves consist
of hollow balls of cells, and are called 'alveoli'. It is here that milk
will be secreted after childbirth.

Each lactiferous duct system forms a lobe of the breast, and each
breast lobe is partially separated from the other lobes by condensa-
tions of tissue which form 'ligaments' in the substance of the breast.

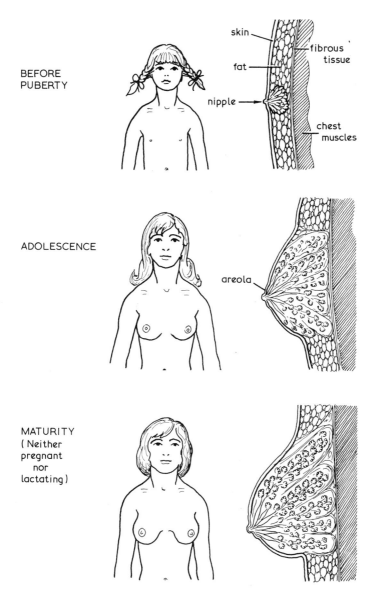

BEFORE PUBERTY

skin

fibrous tissue

fat

nipple

chest muscles

ADOLESCENCE

areola

MATURITY
(Neither pregnant nor lactating)

Fig. 2   The development of the breast from pre-puberty to maturity

The ligaments reach from the fibrous tissue which underlies the breast covering the chest muscles, to the layer of fibrous tissue attached to the skin which covers it. They were first described by a famous surgeon of the early 19th century, Sir Astley Cooper: 'By these processes, the breast is slung upon the forepart of the chest, for they form a moveable but very firm connection with the skin so that the breast has sufficient motion. . . .'

The lobes divide into lobules (the branches and leaves of the tree). The lobules then divide further, so that each lobule is made up of between 30 and 100 milk-producing alveoli, which are small sacs lined with one or two layers of cells (Fig. 3). Fan-shaped cells containing tiny muscles cover each alveolus, like a driving glove covering a hand. Their purpose is to contract when the alveolus is full of milk and, by squeezing, to propel the milk along the ducts towards the nipple. Connective tissue and fat surround each lobule and separate it from its neighbours. Blood vessels, lymph vessels and nerves pass through the connective tissue, supplying the alveoli with blood and lymph. These are the vessels described by Dr Applebaum as the 'interweaving vines and vegetation'.

The size and shape of the breast do not depend upon the number of lobes and lobules, but on the amount of fat deposited in and around them and on the quality of Cooper's ligaments within the breast (Fig. 3). By late adolescence a woman's breasts are firm and conical, but their size varies considerably from one individual to another. As a woman grows older, and particularly if she has been pregnant several times, her breasts usually become softer, more flabby and they may sag. After the menopause, the amounts of sex hormones circulating in a woman's blood are reduced considerably, and her breasts shrink in size and sag increasingly, but a wide variation occurs.

It is important for women to remember that the 'idealized' breasts which appear in magazines such as *Playboy* and *Penthouse*, in 'girlie magazines' and in advertising are usually air-brushed, soft-focus, photo-retouched fantasies. They bear little relationship to the reality. When fully developed, women's breasts are of various shapes and sizes, of varying degree of firmness or pendulousness, and the nipples also vary in size. A woman's belief that her breasts do not conform to the 'ideal' may profoundly affect her image of herself. By being aware of the considerable variety in the size and shape of different women's breasts, this negative view may be eliminated, and she may learn to accept her breasts as part of her body. Of course in a 'mammary-oriented' Western society this acceptance may not be easy to achieve. It is interesting that in a research study, photographs of women's breasts were shown and the observer was asked to estimate

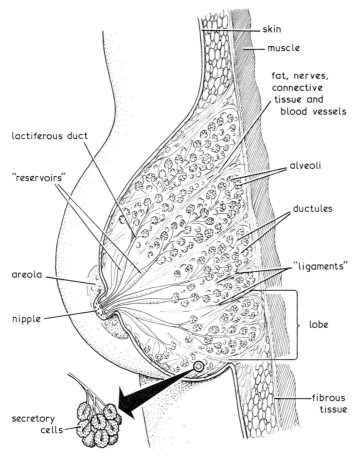

Fig. 3   The mature breast

the age of each woman. The results showed that in many cases it was impossible merely by looking at the photograph to know how old the woman was. This emphasizes the statement that breasts of varying shapes and sizes are normal.

The nipples

Whatever the size and the shape of a woman's breasts, the area around the nipple looks similar in most breasts. The size of the nipple varies: it tends to be larger and more protuberant when a woman has had a baby, and to become smaller in old age. The nipple is surrounded by a disc of thin skin called the areola. Both the nipple and the areola are more deeply pigmented than normal skin, and are relatively hairless. Numbers of tiny smooth muscle fibres are distributed in the substance of each nipple. These contract when stimulated by cold or by sexual arousal to make the nipple erect. The skin of the areola also contains sweat glands and specialized glands. In early pregnancy these specialized glands enlarge to form small bumps on each areola. They are called Montgomery's tubercles after the early 19th-century Irish doctor who first described them. They secrete small quantities of a fatty substance which helps to protect the skin of the areola and nipple during nursing.

Most women are aware that their breasts, and particularly their nipples, vary in sensitivity to touch at different times during the menstrual cycle. The sensitivity of the nipples is greatest at mid-cycle (that is about half way between the menstrual periods) and during menstruation. This sensitivity is due to the influence of the sex hormones but, oddly, in pregnancy, when high levels of hormones circulate in the blood, the sensitivity of the breasts to touch diminishes. Then within 24 hours of childbirth a dramatic increase occurs in the sensitivity of the nipple. This may be an evolutionary device for activating the mother's desire to suckle her baby, which in turn promotes milk production.

The development of a woman's breasts follows no strict timetable. Some girls have well-developed breasts by the age of 13, others have relatively small breasts until they are 16 or 17 years old. The final size of the breasts is just as variable and depends mostly on genetic inheritance. If the girl's mother has large breasts, the chance that her daughter will have large breasts is greater than if her mother has small breasts. The physical size of the girl is not related to the size of her breasts. A slim, small girl may develop big breasts, while a large girl may have small breasts.

By the end of adolescence most women's breasts are fully developed. Their size varies considerably and depends on the quantity of fat rather than on the quantity of gland tissue in the breast. The more fat there is, the greater is the strain on the supporting ligaments, so that big breasts are more likely to sag.

BREAST CHANGES IN THE MENSTRUAL CYCLE

During a woman's reproductive years, from about 13 to 51, the changing quantities of hormones circulating in the blood during the menstrual cycle cause alterations in the size of her breasts. In the first half of the cycle the hormone oestrogen predominates and leads to a growth of the ductules and alveoli; then, after mid-cycle, the hormone progesterone adds its effect by increasing the growth of the alveoli still further. In addition, a variable amount of fluid is retained in the tissues of the breasts, the quantity increasing in the week or 10 days before menstruation. The result of these changes is that most women's breasts increase in size throughout the menstrual cycle. Some women's breasts enlarge by as little as eight per cent, other women's breasts become 44 per cent bigger in the seven to 10 days before menstruation. During this time women find that their breasts become somewhat tender and feel heavier. If the breasts are palpated, the gland tissue in them – which feels 'knobbly' – may be rather more obvious. In a few women these normal changes are so marked that the woman has severe tenderness of her breasts which may become painful.

BREAST CHANGES IN PREGNANCY

In pregnancy the changes which occur in the breasts as menstruation approaches continue in an exaggerated form. The enlargement is due to the sex hormones, oestrogen and progesterone, which are secreted in increasing amounts throughout pregnancy, and probably to a special pregnancy hormone secreted by the placenta and called human placental lactogen (HPL). Oestrogen makes the milk ducts grow and branch, while progesterone induces growth of the milk-producing cells in the alveoli. Human placental lactogen assists progesterone in the development of the alveoli. The hormones also lead to a considerable increase in the size of the blood vessels which supply the breast tissues and carry the extra nutrients essential for the continued growth of the ducts, lobules and alveoli. The dilated veins beneath the skin covering the breasts become prominent. At the same time, fat is deposited around the growing milk-gland systems and a certain amount of fluid is retained in the cells and between them. The result is that the breasts increase in size considerably. The size of a woman's breasts before pregnancy bears no relationship to her ability to breast feed. The critical factor is the amount of gland

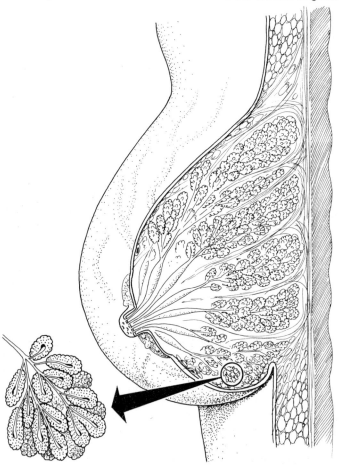

Fig. 4   The breast in pregnancy. Insert drawing shows an alveolus

tissue in her breasts. Small breasts may contain more milk-gland tissue than big breasts, but, of course, less fat.

Most pregnant women's breasts have reached their maximum size (that is until the milk 'comes in' after childbirth) by the beginning of the last quarter of pregnancy (Fig. 4). By this stage most women feel more comfortable if they buy bras two or three sizes larger than normal or, preferably, a correctly fitted maternity bra.

THE BENEFITS OF BREAST MILK

A human baby, up to the time he is six months old and often longer, can be fed in one of two ways. His mother can choose to breast feed him; or she can give him a 'modified' cow's milk from a bottle – in other words, feed him artificially on formula milk.

The evidence is that human milk is the most appropriate, nutritiously balanced, 'protective' food for the growth and development of a human baby. Cow's milk, however modified or adapted in formula preparations, is never as good as human milk, although babies will thrive on formula milk, as long as it is prepared properly and hygienically, if the mother is unable to breast feed her baby.

All mammalian milks are nutritionally balanced foods. That is to say that they contain protein, for tissue growth and repair; carbohydrate, as milk sugar, for energy; and fats, which provide energy and supply 'coating' for the rapidly growing brain cells and connecting fibres of young babies. All milks also contain vitamins, minerals and trace elements. However, the proportion of each of these constituents varies, depending on the species, and human breast milk is no exception.

As shown in Table 1, the composition of human and cow's milk differs, and a particularly important difference occurs in the protein content. Milk proteins consist of casein and whey proteins. The proportion of these two protein groups is reversed in human and cow's milk, cow's milk containing more casein and less whey than human milk. Inside a baby's stomach the casein clots to form curds, the whey remaining liquid (curds and whey). Because cow's milk contains so much casein more curds are formed and the curd is tough and rubbery. It stays longer in a baby's stomach, but once it gets into the baby's intestines it passes through them rapidly, so that less of the nutrient, casein, is absorbed. The slow emptying from the baby's stomach of cow's milk curd has an implication in infant feeding. Babies fed formula milk based on cow's milk only want to be fed every three or four hours, because their stomachs are full for this time, but breast-fed babies, whose stomachs empty more quickly, generally need to be fed at shorter intervals.

Table 1   Composition of human milk and cow's milk

BIOCHEMICAL SUBSTANCE	HUMAN MILK	COW'S MILK
Water per 100ml	87.1	87.3
Total solids – g/100ml		
Protein	0.9	3.3
Casein – % of total	20	82
Whey – % of total	80	18
Fat	4.5	3.7
Milk sugar – lactose	6.8	4.8
Minerals – mg/100ml		
Calcium – mg	34	125
Phosphorus – mg	14	96
Sodium – mmol/litre	7	25
Vitamins per 100ml		
vitamin Aiu	190	100
vitamin B_1iu	16	44
vitamin B_2iu	36	175
vitamin Biu	150	950
vitamin Cmg	43	11
Energy provided – kcal/100ml	75	69

Human milk curd is soft and flocculent, and the relatively high proportion of whey enables the baby to absorb milk protein more easily. The proteins in the whey of human milk provide anti-infective substances which protect breast-fed babies against infection. Human milk lacks a substance contained in cow's milk called beta-lacto-globulin, which may cause milk allergies in small formula-fed babies.

Human milk also contains more of the milk sugar lactose than cow's milk. Lactose has two benefits: first it is a ready source of energy, and second it helps calcium absorption by the baby. Calcium is needed to make growing bones strong. Lactose also promotes the multiplication of bacteria in the baby's gut. The bacteria produce a weak acid which discourages the growth of those bacteria which cause gastro-enteritis.

Although cow's milk contains more fat than human milk, the fat is less easily absorbed by the baby and so provides less energy. This is because human milk contains an enzyme, lipase, which is not found in cow's milk. Lipase has the effect of starting the breakdown of the fats with the release of fatty acids in the baby's intestines, so that the fats are partially digested before being absorbed. In addition to providing energy for the baby, fatty acids, particularly long-chain fatty acids, are involved in the development of the brain and are present in higher concentration in human milk than in cow's milk.

It might be thought that in one way cow's milk is superior to breast milk because it contains nearly four times as much calcium (1250mg per litre) as human milk (340mg per litre). A lack of calcium in the blood may cause convulsions or tetany. Surprisingly, bottle-fed babies are more likely to show signs of calcium deficiency in the first three weeks of their life than are breast-fed babies. There are two reasons for this. The first is that some bottle-fed babies fail to absorb the calcium from the formula milk because it is precipitated in the baby's intestines by fatty acids which are released by the action of intestinal enzymes on the fat in cow's milk. The resulting mixture is like a soap. The calcium is firmly bound and cannot be extracted to be absorbed into the baby's intestines. A second reason is that cow's milk contains a higher level of phosphorus than human milk. Phosphorus competes with calcium to be absorbed. The effect of these two mechanisms is that although cow's milk contains more calcium than breast milk, less is absorbed, and low blood levels of calcium may result. This may be the cause of convulsions, which affect about one bottle-fed baby in every 100. Fortunately the problem is self-limiting, and after the first month of life most formula-fed babies drink sufficient milk each day to raise their blood levels of calcium to normal.

Although the amount of iron in human and cow's milk is approximately the same (0.5–1.5mg per litre), the baby absorbs more iron from breast milk than from cow's milk. Nearly half the iron available in human milk is absorbed by the baby, compared with only about 10 per cent of the iron in cow's milk. Manufacturers of formula milks are aware of this fact and add extra iron (12–18mg per litre) to their formulations of cow's milk.

THE BENEFITS OF BREAST FEEDING FOR THE MOTHER

It should be stated at the outset that many of the advantages of breast feeding for the mother will also be obtained if a formula-fed baby is cared for as intensively as is a breast-fed baby. Unfortunately, sometimes this does not occur; also, breast feeding does confer some additional benefits on the mother (Table 2).

In the first place, breast feeding increases the interaction or attachment between the mother and her baby. This interaction has been recognized recently as important in the child's development. Second, breast feeding has been shown to improve the skills of mothering. These two benefits relate to the mother and her baby. Third, breast feeding benefits the mother directly, as women who choose to breast feed regain their figures more quickly than women who choose to bottle feed. Finally, breast feeding is more convenient than bottle feeding, or would be if society were more supportive of breast feeding.

Mother–baby interaction

Recently, scientists have recognized that a newborn baby is not a passive, reflecting, inert organism, but a complex individual who responds to stimuli with an amazing alertness and to a far greater extent than had been appreciated.

In the first minutes, or hours, after birth, if the baby is given to its mother for most of the time, he learns to recognize her smell, her touch and perhaps her appearance. After the first two weeks of life this extraordinary responsiveness diminishes, returning more slowly during the first year.

When a baby and its mother are in close contact for most of the time during the first days of its life, 'bonding' occurs between them. Bonding is enhanced by breast feeding and probably leads to an increased maternal affection over the first year of life. Fairly continuous early contact also seems to improve the baby's patterns of sleeping, waking and crying, although there are wide variations between babies. A baby who has early contact with its mother and who 'rooms in' with her, spending all, or nearly all, its time with her, generally cries less, establishes a day–night rhythm of wakefulness and sleep more quickly than babies who are kept in nurseries, cared for by several different people and fed at a three- or four-hourly routine.

Mothering

Mothering involves more than feeding the baby and changing his nappies! It involves body contact, warmth, comfort, soothing and

Table 2   The benefits of breast feeding

- Breast feeding enables the mother and baby to interact more fully than bottle feeding. This interaction, or 'bonding', may be a factor in the observed increased intelligence of breast-fed babies tested up to the age of 15.

- Breast milk supplies substances which protect the baby against infections, especially gastro-intestinal infections, respiratory infections and viral infections. Although such infections are uncommon in the industrialized nations, they do occur, and they are common in the Third World.

- Breast milk, to a large degree, protects babies against allergic disorders, especially asthma and eczema. For example, an investigation in England showed that of 300 allergic children aged 4 to 14, no child had developed eczema while being exclusively breast fed.

- Breast-fed babies are less likely to become obese, which if it persists is a factor in adult life of coronary heart disease, high blood pressure, gall bladder disease and diabetes.

- Breast-fed babies do not develop high blood levels of salt, or become dehydrated. This may occur in bottle-fed babies if the formula is incorrectly mixed, and many are, as a survey in London in 1975 showed. In that investigation one mother in five was making up the feed in a way which was 'seriously incorrect'. If a baby retains excessive salt and becomes dehydrated his brain may be damaged.

- Breast feeding is more convenient for the mother. If she bottle feeds, unless she has help, she has to mix the formula feed, sterilize the bottles and teats, warm the mixture, feed her baby, wash out and resterilize the bottle and teat. If she breast feeds she only has to give her breast to her baby to suck.

- Finally, breast feeding costs less than bottle feeding, although this factor is unlikely to influence a woman's choice.

interaction between the mother and her baby. While breast feeding does not guarantee good mothering, nor formula feeding prevent it, in general, the conditions needed for breast feeding increase the physical contact between mother and baby and enhance mothering skills (Fig. 5).

Breast feeding is also an erotic experience, which is increased by skin-to-skin contact as the baby nuzzles the breast. The reflex which engorges the nipple to make it erect is similar to the reflex which

Fig. 5   Breast feeding – note the eye-to-eye contact of mother and baby

engorges the genital tissues when stimulated directly or by fantasy. A baby suckling at the breast induces the same reflex as a lover sucking, and a few women have orgasms when breast feeding. The milk 'let-down' reflex is controlled by the hormone oxytocin, which also makes the uterus contract (see p. 33). Enjoyable nursing, like enjoyable sex, is liberating, and increases the sensitivity with which a mother responds. The erotic nature of breast feeding is further suggested by the observation that more women who breast feed have an earlier and stronger return of sexual desire and response than do women who choose to formula feed.

In addition to the erotic nature of breast feeding, many mothers discover an emotional contentment in handling their baby during breast feeding and in the close body contact which breast feeding necessarily entails. A bottle-fed baby can receive all his nourishment held in one position, his head cradled in his mother's arms and watched by his mother, but without much body contact. A breast-fed baby is in a closer physical relationship with his mother as she offers him her breast, adjusting her body to his so that he can suckle easily and breathe at the same time. His hands can wander, touching her, and she moves him across her body to suckle at her other breast. She and her baby are in close physical contact, which is known to increase emotional contact. The co-operative act of breast feeding encourages co-operation and emotional exchange between the two which may have a beneficial effect on the behaviour of the child when it becomes an adult.

Restoration of the figure

During pregnancy most women in Western countries lay down between three and four kilograms (6–8lb) of fat. If a woman wants to regain her pre-pregnancy figure, this stored energy has to be used up. A woman who chooses to breast feed will use up the stored energy more quickly than a woman who chooses to bottle feed, and will thus regain her pre-pregnancy figure more quickly. It is true that her breasts will remain larger for longer, but there is no evidence that at the end of breast feeding her breasts will necessarily be less firm and conical than those of a woman who did not breast feed.

Convenience

The convenience of breast feeding is obvious. There is no need to clean, sterilize and store feeding bottles and teats. There is no need to prepare the formula milk and to warm it to the right temperature before a feed.

At night, a nursing mother merely has to reach out, pick up and cuddle her baby in the crook of her arm and let him feed. She does not have to get out of bed to prepare the feed. She just turns on her side and lets her baby suckle her nipple. As Dr Jelliffe has written: 'In the present day world's dietary patterns, the stress is increasingly on convenience foods, that is processed foods that are precooked and ready to eat, possibly after initial warming. . . . Human milk represents the original ready-to-serve 24-hour convenience food, with advantages for both the father and the nursing mother.'

THE INITIATION OF LACTATION

The gland tissue of the breasts reaches its maximum size by the middle of pregnancy and from this time on small amounts of colostrum begin to be secreted in the milk-producing alveoli and may be expressed from the nipple. Colostrum is the milk-like fluid which is secreted before the milk is made.

Milk is not produced until after the baby has been born, when secretion begins because of the effect of the hormone prolactin on the milk-producing alveolar cells.

Prolactin is secreted during pregnancy by specialized cells in the front part of the pituitary gland, the amount secreted rising as pregnancy advances, until at the end of pregnancy the level is high (Fig. 6). This level is sufficient to induce milk production in the breasts. However, lactation does not occur because prolactin is 'blocked' from acting on the milk-producing alveolar cells of the breasts by the high levels of oestrogen and the second sex hormone, progesterone, which are produced by the placenta and circulate in the woman's blood. These hormones occupy 'receptor sites' on the surface of the cells, preventing prolactin from entering the cell (Figs. 7(a) and (b)).

Within two days of the birth of the baby (and the expulsion of the placenta) the blood levels of oestrogen and progesterone have fallen sufficiently to enable prolactin to enter the alveolar cells, which begin to synthesize and to secrete milk, with the result that the breasts become heavier and fuller (Fig. 8).

The sooner after birth a mother suckles the baby, and within reason the more often he suckles at her breasts, the more prolactin is secreted and the more milk is produced. This is because of the prolactin reflex. Suckling, or other nipple stimulation, provokes messages which are transmitted along the nerves to the brain where

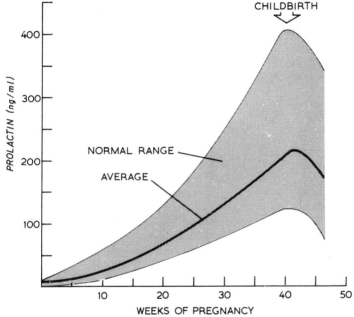

Fig. 6   Prolactin concentrations in blood during pregnancy

they cause the release of a surge of prolactin. The prolactin acts on the alveoli of the breasts with the result that they become refilled with milk in the two to three hours after a feed and, once milk secretion is established, automatically adjust the amount made to the amount taken by the baby (Fig. 9).

The prolactin reflex is influenced by many factors. If a woman is anxious about her ability to feed, or embarrassed about exposing her breasts, or if she finds it painful when the baby suckles, the

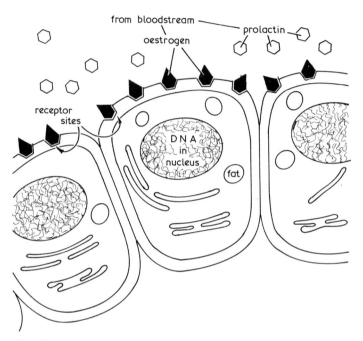

Fig. 7(a)   In pregnancy *receptor sites occupied by oestrogen:*
prolactin unable to bind on to the sites and enter the
alveolar epithelial cell

release of prolactin may be inhibited and milk secretion may diminish. On the other hand, if a woman is relaxed, happy, free from pain
and confident about breast feeding, prolactin secretion is increased.
However, the most important stimulus to the prolactin reflex is the
baby's ability to suckle.

Once lactation has started, the alveolar cells secrete milk continu-
ously. Between feeds this accumulates in the milk-producing sacs
and in the smaller ducts in the lobules. A mother may give her baby
200ml at each feed, which means that each breast holds about 100ml
of milk in the alveoli and the ductules.

As long as a mother continues to breast feed, the prolactin reflex
will go on working, and the level of prolactin in her blood will remain
high. It is highest in the first 12 weeks after the birth of the baby and

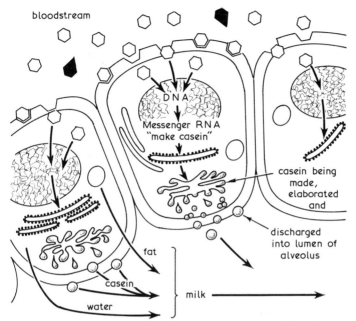

bloodstream

D N A

Messenger RNA "make casein"

casein being made, elaborated and

discharged into lumen of alveolus

fat

casein

water

milk ⟶

Fig. 7(b) Following childbirth *the level of oestrogen falls and prolactin is able to enter the alveolar epithelial cell and initiate milk secretion*

then drops to some extent, but remains above the level found in the blood of women who choose not to breast feed.

Prolactin causes the milk-secreting alveoli to fill, but the hormone has no effect in helping the milk move from the alveoli deep in the breasts and flow along the branching ducts until it reaches the nipple and becomes available for the baby. In other words, the milk is of no value to the baby until it has been ejected from the alveoli and has been 'let-down' through the ducts. Milk ejection, or 'let-down', is also due to a reflex. It works in this way. The milk-producing alveoli in the breasts are surrounded by tiny muscle fibres (Fig. 10). When these fibres contract they squeeze the milk out of the sacs and propel it along the branching ducts until it reaches the main duct from that breast lobule and passes along it to the nipple.

The milk-ejection or 'let-down' reflex is initiated by nerve impulses

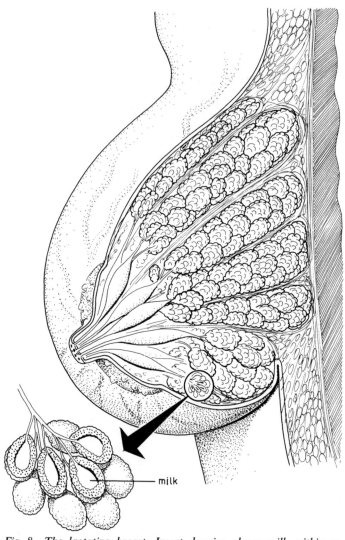

milk

Fig. 8 *The lactating breast. Insert drawing shows milk within an alveolus*

passing to the brain from the nipple and areola, when they are stimulated by the baby suckling. The nerve impulses reach the pituitary gland, which secretes a hormone called oxytocin. Oxytocin is released into the bloodstream and carried to the breasts, where it makes the tiny muscle network (called myo-epithelial cells) surrounding the alveoli contract. The contraction of the myo-epithelial cells squeezes the milk out of the alveoli and ejects it, or 'lets it down', into the dilated part of the main ducts which lie beneath the areola (Fig. 11). Oxytocin also increases the blood flow through the

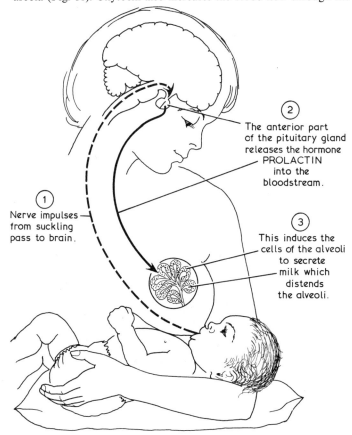

(2) The anterior part of the pituitary gland releases the hormone PROLACTIN into the bloodstream.

(1) Nerve impulses from suckling pass to brain.

(3) This induces the cells of the alveoli to secrete milk which distends the alveoli.

Fig. 9   The prolactin reflex

breasts, bringing additional nutrients for the alveolar cells to produce more milk.

The 'let-down' reflex is helped or hindered by psychological influences. It is helped if the mother is relaxed and confident, if she is free from pain and if she is not embarrassed about breast feeding. It is hindered if the woman is anxious or in pain, or if her baby doesn't suck strongly. If the 'let-down' reflex is inhibited or hindered, the baby sucks without getting much milk, and the milk it gets is relatively poor in quality. Because the baby is hungry he cries continually, which increases the mother's anxiety. At the same time her engorged breasts become painful. Anxious about her ability to feed, her engorged breasts painful, she approaches the next feed with anxiety. At the next feed the engorgement of her breasts reduces the protractility of her nipples and the baby finds it harder to suckle.

The combination of poor suckling, which reduces the prolactin reflex, and the distension of the alveoli by milk which has not been 'let-down', reduces the secretion of new milk. Poor suckling also inhibits the release of oxytocin to start the 'let-down' reflex. The result is that the baby continues to cry from hunger; the mother becomes increasingly anxious and her breasts become increasingly painful, particularly as her hungry baby may bite on her nipples, which then become painful or cracked.

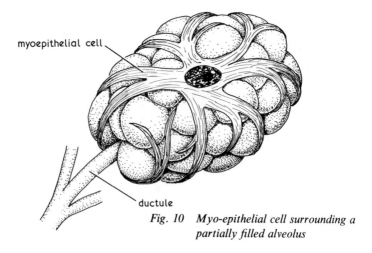

myoepithelial cell

ductule

Fig. 10   Myo-epithelial cell surrounding a partially filled alveolus

The mother has lost her confidence. She has inhibited her 'let-down' reflex and her baby is hungry. She interprets this as 'I have insufficient milk and it doesn't suit the baby.' She abandons breast feeding.

This sequence explains why successful breast feeding is a 'confidence trick'. A confident mother will not inhibit her 'let-down' reflex. In fact, a woman who is confident about breast feeding often ejects

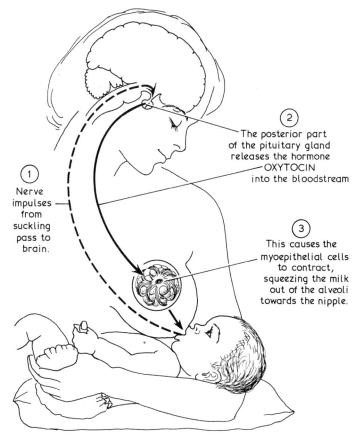

② The posterior part of the pituitary gland releases the hormone OXYTOCIN into the bloodstream

① Nerve impulses from suckling pass to brain.

③ This causes the myoepithelial cells to contract, squeezing the milk out of the alveoli towards the nipple.

Fig. 11   The milk ejection ('let-down') reflex

milk from her breasts when she hears her baby cry, or when she
thinks about feeding him.

THE PREPARATION OF THE BREASTS
IN PREGNANCY

There are several simple things a woman should do during pregnancy
to prepare for breast feeding. Some of these help to prepare her
nipples, others help to make her breasts comfortable.

Nipple care

During pregnancy the nipples become protractile, and the areola
develops. The aim of nipple care is to make the nipples soft and
'rubbery', and to give the woman confidence about touching and
handling her nipples and her breasts. When she baths or showers she
should wash her nipples (preferably avoiding the use of soap, which
removes the natural skin oils). Many women rub in a small amount
of anhydrous lanolin (wool fat) after drying their nipples and areolae
to replace the natural skin fats. Another method of preventing the
skin of the areola and the nipples from damage when lactation is
established is to expose the breasts to the air, or to sunbathe for a
period every day.

Unless the woman has inverted nipples, when she should draw
them out each day, she needs do nothing else to them. She should
avoid scrubbing them with a nail brush, or putting alcohol on them,
as these old-fashioned ideas have been shown to increase rather than
reduce the chance of getting cracked nipples.

Breast care

Most women find it more comfortable to wear a bra from about
mid-pregnancy but whether or not you wear a bra is your decision.
If you choose to use one it is best to buy a maternity bra, which is
designed to give maximum support to the heavier breasts.

A number of doctors recommend that from the 30th week of
pregnancy, women should massage their breasts gently (Fig. 12). To
do this they place their open hands at the periphery of each
breast, and move them towards the areola pressing gently. Once

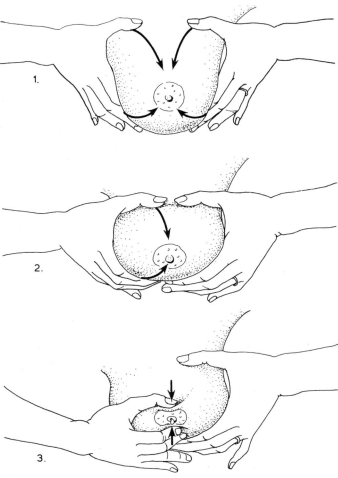

Fig. 12   Breast hand-massage. (1) How the hands are placed at the
start of expression to enclose the breast at its margin; (2)
The hands move inwards towards the areola, firm pressure
being exerted on the whole breast. The movement is
repeated about 5 to 10 times; (3) The breast is fixed by one
hand and the milk ducts are compressed with the other
hand, the thumb above and the fingers below. The pressure
empties the milk ducts. At the end of the expression, the
nipple is drawn out with the fingers

this has been done, a woman should try to express colostrum from the dilated part of the main milk ducts, as they lie beneath the areola.

There is some doubt about the value of breast expression, some doctors believing it to be of no value in opening the ducts. But it has the advantage of giving a woman confidence in touching and handling her breasts, and more intimate knowledge about her body. If you choose to practise breast expression, this is how to go about it. Place your thumb at the edge of the areola above your nipple and your first finger at the edge of the areola underneath your nipple. With your other fingers support your breast. It will be clear from this description that when hand-expressing your left breast you use your right hand and when you express your right breast you use your left hand. A good place to do hand-expression is under a shower when your breasts are wet.

If you feel gently (that is 'palpate': the word means just that) around the edge of the areola and under it you will notice small firm areas under your fingers. These are the dilated part of the ducts. Pressing inwards and towards your nipple, squeeze gently between finger and thumb, and beads of colostrum will appear on your nipple.

The first time you hand-express you may not obtain any colostrum – don't worry, try again. Although a few women are unable to express colostrum, most will find that it appears as a lemon-yellow bead on the nipple. Above all be gentle, don't hurt yourself. If you do, you are not expressing properly.

Of course, there is another way to stimulate your breasts. This is when making love. Your husband or partner can hand-express or suck your breasts, if you and he get enjoyment from doing this. It has the advantage that he becomes involved in your preparation for feeding the baby he has fathered.

The idea is that expressing the breasts in this way will open the ducts and prepare them for the flow of milk after childbirth.

INVERTED NIPPLES IN PREGNANCY

In pregnancy, the nipples increase in size, and become more 'protractile', which will enable the baby to fit the nipple into his mouth and stretch it to the back of his hard palate more effectively.

One woman in every five has nipples which are not fully pro-protractile, probably because the nipple, instead of being loosely attached to the breast tissues, is more adherent to the underlying structures (Fig. 13). The baby usually breaks the adhesions when he sucks at the breast, but this is rather uncomfortable for the mother and may hinder the smooth establishment of lactation. The condition is called 'pseudo inversion of the nipples'. A woman can tell if she

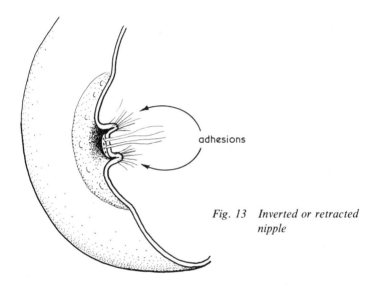

adhesions

Fig. 13   Inverted or retracted nipple

has pseudo inversion by doing the 'thumb test' (Fig. 14). The nipple looks normal, but when she presses the edge of the areola between her fingers and thumb, instead of the nipple remaining protractile it retracts into the breast tissue. If a woman has pseudo-inverted nipples she should do specific exercises in the second half of pregnancy to break the adhesions. Several times a day, she should place her opposing thumbs, one on each side of her nipple, in the horizontal plane and draw on the areola by moving her thumbs outward (Fig. 15). She should repeat the exercise a few times and then move her thumbs to the vertical plane, so that one thumb is above the nipple and one below, and do the exercise again. As the nipple is stimulated and protracts, the adhesions at the base of the nipple are

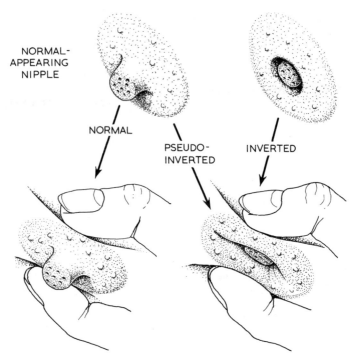

NORMAL-
APPEARING
NIPPLE

NORMAL

PSEUDO-
INVERTED

INVERTED

Fig. 14   The thumb test for inverted or pseudo-inverted nipples

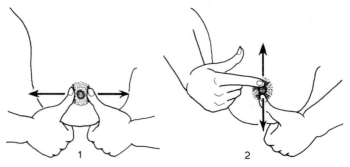

1

2

Fig. 15   A method of treating inverted nipples in pregnancy

stretched and broken. A pleasant way of helping the nipples to become protractile is for the woman's husband (or partner) to stimulate them with his fingers, and to suck them gently during fore-play.

A few women have completely inverted nipples. When the woman looks at her breasts, the nipple is represented by a pit. The exercise mentioned may help the nipples to become protractile, but usually plastic nipple shields, which are worn under the bra, are needed to 'draw out' the nipples. The shields are hollow and saucer-shaped with a hole in the middle which is placed over the nipple (Fig. 16). The shields put continuous pressure around the areola, which encourages the nipple to become protractile inside the hollow.

A woman who has inverted nipples should start wearing the shields about half way through pregnancy. She should wear them initially for an hour or two each day and gradually increase the time until she is wearing them all day without discomfort. If they hurt she should take them out of her bra and give her breasts a rest! They should not be worn at night.

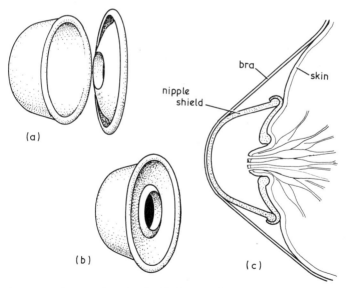

Fig. 16   The use of nipple shields for completely inverted nipples

Some women find that colostrum leaks from the nipples inside the nipple shield. Colostrum may moisten the nipples leading to soreness. To prevent this a small towelling nursing pad can be placed inside the shield to absorb the moisture and the nipples should be covered with anhydrous lanolin to 'waterproof' them.

Most women do not find the plastic shields uncomfortable, because during pregnancy the sensitivity of the nipples diminishes. Immediately the baby is born there is a considerable increase in the sensitivity of the nipples; this is important so that messages from the sensitive nipples can reach the brain when the baby sucks, to initiate the 'let-down' reflex.

LEARNING TO BREAST FEED SUCCESSFULLY

Successful breast feeding is achieved if the mother is confident about her ability to breast feed, if she is helped to establish lactation by informed, experienced health professionals, and if she is able to obtain support when she returns home. This support has been called 'mothering the mother'. She needs to have some person or organization to whom she can turn, from whom she can ask questions and who will give her honest answers. Successful breast feeding is best learned by watching someone else breast feed . . . and then by practice. It cannot be learned by reading books, although books can help mothers to develop the required confidence.

The baby also has to learn to breast feed. He has a 'rooting' reflex, which means that he turns towards the breast of whoever holds him and 'roots' in search of milk. The rooting reflex is not always well developed and some babies seem to reject their mothers. Of course, they don't really, they just need encouragement and help.

We don't know how the rooting reflex starts, but probably pressure on a baby's cheek, or the smell and warmth of being cuddled, send a message to its brain, and the baby turns its face towards where it thinks the breast is, opening and shutting its mouth, as if searching for a nipple.

The first days after your baby has been born is a learning time for both of you. Because of this you must not be discouraged if everything doesn't go perfectly at first.

This is how the Nursing Mothers' Association of Australia suggests you go about learning to breast feed:

- Be relaxed and happy, and give yourself time to enjoy touching, looking at, cuddling and getting to know your baby.

- When your baby tells you he wants to be fed, wash your hands and unfasten your bra. Make sure you are comfortable and relaxed, whether in bed with pillows behind you and one under your knees, or lying on your side in bed, or on a chair with your feet on a low stool or cushion (Fig. 17). You may like a cushion on your lap to support baby. You, and only you, can find the position which is most comfortable and convenient for you to feed your baby. If you are not comfortable, your baby will sense it and won't have the security he needs.

- Lift him from the bassinet and, if he is wrapped up, release him so that his arms and hands are free to explore, to wave, to touch the breast or hold your finger. Cuddle him for a moment, so that he can 'recognize' your touch and smell. This is important if he is upset or crying.

- Lift your breast clear of your bra and squeeze a drop or two of colostrum on to your nipple for your baby to smell and taste. This encourages him to suckle (Fig. 18).

- With your first and middle fingers supporting the nipple from just outside the areola, touch the nipple against your baby's cheek and, as he instinctively turns his head towards it, slip it in-to his mouth. You may have to repeat this a couple of times if the nipple slips out of his mouth. The baby's mouth must be right over the nipple and well on to the surrounding areola. He must be able to breathe through his nose while he sucks, so you may need to press the breast clear of his nose with your finger (Fig. 19). You can also support the breast a little with your hand so that all the milk will flow from the lower part of the breast. If your baby is sleepy, coax him gently on to the breast. Don't force him if he is not hungry. You can express now and try again later.

- If he is sleepy and doesn't seem to want to suckle he will usually become more alert if you rub your nipple to and fro across his lips, or press his cheek against your breast. It is not a good idea to shake, pinch or prod a sleepy baby, as he may associate this with sucking your breast and decide he doesn't like either.

- Both breasts should be offered to your baby at each feed. Give

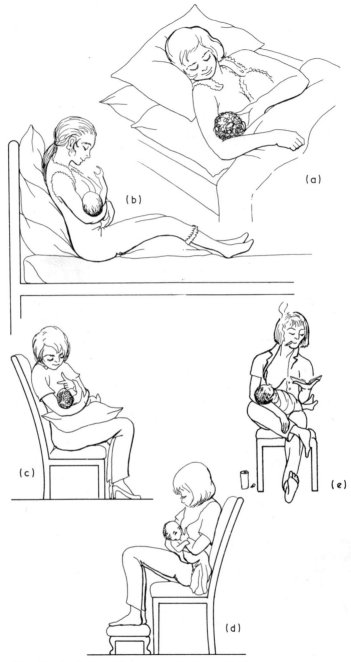

Fig. 17 (a–d) Suitable positions for breast feeding – mother comfortable and eye-to-eye contact with baby; (e) Never!

Fig. 18   Breast feeding – squeezing colostrum on to the nipple to encourage the baby to suckle

the right breast first at one feed, and the left breast first at the next feed. When you feed from the left breast, cradle him in your left arm. With your right hand, support your breast, with your first finger and thumb flat above and your middle finger below the areola. Using these fingers you can make sure that your breast doesn't fall over his nose and obstruct his breathing. You can also make sure that he takes your nipple and most of the areola well inside his mouth. By pressing gently on the areola,

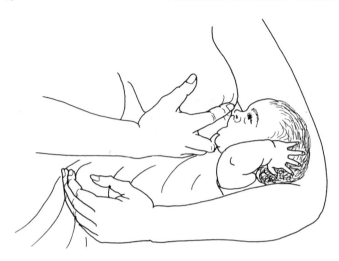

Fig. 19   Technique of breast feeding. Note how the mother
holds the baby, pressing her breast tissue with the index
finger so that the baby can breathe easily

you can encourage the milk to eject into his mouth, although in
fact the baby does nearly all the work!

For convenience in communication, a baby is said to 'suck' milk
from the breast. In fact, suction only plays a small part in transfer-
ring milk from a mother's breast to her baby. Most of the transfer is
effected by an intermittent squeezing of the dilated part of the milk
ducts beneath the areola by the baby's chewing action. This causes
the milk to squirt out of the several tiny openings in the nipple, just
as milk squirts out of a cow's teats when she is milked.

It is for this reason that a mother must make sure that her nipple
is well inside the baby's mouth, so that the dilated parts of the milk
ducts are between his upper and lower jaws (Fig. 20). His jaws 'chew'
on the dilated ducts, not on the nipple, and it is this chewing action
together with the pad of his tongue, which protrudes out over his
lower jaw and makes a vacuum, which help the suction needed for
the milk to squirt into his mouth. The further back in his mouth
that the nipple is placed, the less will it be rubbed by his tongue as
he sucks, and the less it will be hurt by his chewing jaws. You can

prove this by putting your thumb in your mouth, and sucking it. The deeper it is inside your mouth, the less its end is rubbed.

It is important to make a clear distinction between sucking and suckling. A baby sucks milk from a bottle, but he suckles at the breast, grasping the milk 'reservoirs' between his lips and tongue, and pressing on the nipple with his tongue and his hard palate. This action seals his oral cavity, and the action of muscles in his cheeks creates a negative pressure in his mouth which encourages the milk flow.

This effect can be proved when a mother wants to take her baby

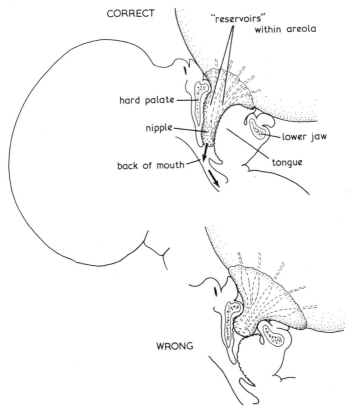

Fig. 20   Ideal position of the nipple in the baby's mouth

off her breast. She doesn't just pull him off. If she does she will get sore nipples and an angry baby. All that she has to do to avoid these problems is to insert a finger into the corner of the baby's mouth to break the vacuum, and he can then be detached from the nipple quite easily (Fig. 21).

A certain amount of nipple tenderness is not unusual in the first days of breast feeding, but it can be minimized by following the techniques we have been discussing.

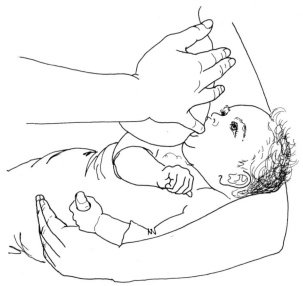

Fig. 21   How the mother releases her nipple from the baby's mouth

ENCOURAGING LACTATION

Frequent short feeds are the best way of getting the milk to 'come in'. Don't let the excuse of hospital routine prevent you from feeding often. It is your baby, and the hospital staff are there to help you (Table 3).

During the first three or four days before the milk 'comes in' each feed should be short, lasting a few minutes at each breast, but repeated often.

The first attempt at feeding should be immediately after your baby is born. After that you should cuddle your baby and put him to your breast at intervals so that he may learn its smell and touch. He will not want milk at this stage, and he will sleep most of the time, but give him your breast whenever you or he want to and at least every three hours. The length of time the baby suckles varies, depending how you and your baby interact. The older method of feeding for a fixed number of minutes (three minutes each feed on the first day, then five, seven and 10 minutes on subsequent days) has been shown to be less effective in establishing lactation. Unlimited suckling is not associated with an increase in sore nipples.

Table 3   How to breast feed successfully

- Learn about breast feeding in the weeks before your baby is born.

- Remember that the earlier after birth that you suckle your baby (preferably immediately he is born), the sooner the milk 'comes in' and lactation is established.

- Remember that frequent short periods (lasting about five minutes) of suckling help to bring the milk in and once lactation is established increase the milk supply.

- Try to be relaxed and confident about your ability to breast feed. This stimulates your 'let-down' reflex.

- Insist (after talking with your doctor) that the nursing staff let your baby remain with you, in or beside your bed, so that you can cuddle and feed him when you think he wants to be fed.

- Insist that no glucose water or supplementary feeds are given to your baby without your permission and that of your doctor. Newborn babies rarely need supplementary feedings and if given particularly by bottle, they jeopardize the smooth establishment of lactation.

During this time, the baby should not be given supplementary feeds, especially if given by bottle, as these feeds will reduce his desire to suckle and reduce the prolactin reflex. If it is necessary to give the baby extra fluids (for example if the weather is very hot), insist that you have the opportunity to discuss the matter first and

Table 4   Myths and facts about breast feeding

THE MYTH	THE FACT
Bottle feeding is easier than breast feeding.	It is, if someone else prepares the feed and cleans up afterwards.
You can't tell how much a breast-fed baby gets, but you know how much you have given a bottle-fed baby.	This is partially true. But if the breast-fed baby is contented and thriving he is getting enough. And many bottle-fed babies are overfed or fed on improperly prepared formula feeds – too strong, too weak, or with the wrong quantity of sugar.
Breast feeding makes you more tired than bottle feeding.	Although breast-fed babies need to be fed at more frequent intervals than bottle-fed babies, bottle feeding requires time to prepare the formula, and to clean up the bottles and teat after each feed.
If you breast feed you will get sore nipples or mastitis.	This is a fair comment, but they can be avoided by good prenatal care of the nipples and breasts and by the proper management of the first days after childbirth when lactation is established.
Breast feeding spoils your figure.	The extra fat which is laid down during pregnancy is burnt up if you breast feed; if you choose to bottle feed, the fat may remain.

that the baby is given water by a spoon or dropper rather than by bottle. A baby sucks a bottle differently from how he suckles the breast and may become confused if offered both methods. Once breast feeding has been fully established, the pattern of suckling is fixed, and if you wish to go out it will be all right to give the baby expressed breast milk from a bottle.

Once your milk has 'come in', your baby should be fed at his request. This is called 'demand feeding' or preferably 'need feeding'. The baby knows when he is hungry, more than anyone else. He knows when he needs food. The precise interval is quite unimportant; he can't yet tell the time, and he will find his own rhythm. Some babies want to be fed every three or four hours including during the night, but many want to be fed more often.

In the early weeks of the baby's life, you will have to be prepared to adapt to his needs, feeding him when he wakes up and calls for food. But as he grows older you can start moulding him to your needs, and many babies quickly adjust to a three-or four-hourly schedule. But not all do. Babies who want to be fed more often are not sick or underfed, provided that they are contented and seem to be gaining weight; they have found their own pattern, and there is a lot of evidence that babies, like the young of some other mammals, enjoy frequent feeds.

PART TWO

Questions breast-feeding mothers ask

The Nursing Mothers' Association of Australia (NMAA) is a voluntary helping organization which started in 1964 with six members; today it has over 57 000.

As one of its activities the NMAA has a 24-hour telephone counselling service. This section is based on information obtained from counsellors and in discussions with other nursing organizations, with paediatricians and in response to letters.

AFTER-PAINS

Why do some women get 'after-pains' when they breast feed?

The 'let-down' of milk is due to the release of the hormone oxytocin by the pituitary gland in response to the baby suckling at the breast. Oxytocin also makes the uterus contract, particularly in the first days after childbirth. After-pains are due to uterine contractions, caused by oxytocin released by the 'let-down' reflex. If they are distressing, aspirin will help. Aspirin counteracts the sequence of events (which includes prostaglandin) started by the action of oxytocin on the uterus; if the after-pains are very severe, one of the antiprostaglandin drugs (such as Ponstan) may be prescribed.

BABY, ADOPTED: BREAST FEEDING

Can a woman breast feed an adopted baby?

A number of drugs are now available which increase the secretion and release of prolactin (see p. 150). If the use of these drugs is combined with breast stimulation and sucking by the woman's husband or partner it is possible for some women about to adopt a baby to initiate lactation, which can then be maintained by the baby if the woman 'demand feeds' him, although often supplementary feeds are also needed. Breast feeding is likely to be more successful if the adopting mother has breast fed a baby previously.

Two problems arise. The first is the long delay between registering as an adoptive parent and receiving the baby. This interval is now as long as seven years in Australia and Britain, and the exact date of the baby's arrival often cannot be determined as the natural mother has the right to change her mind about giving her baby for adoption after its birth. This means that drug and stimulatory preparation for lactating may have to be repeated, as the most successful preparation takes two to three months.

The second problem is that the procedure between the birth of the baby and its adoption may take some time. During the period the baby is usually formula fed, and may become so accustomed to the shape and taste of the teat and the taste of cow's milk that he resists the change to suckling at his adopting mother's breast. His resistance may increase when he finds that at first she only secretes small amounts of milk. This is because her prolactin levels are likely to be lower than those of women who have given birth recently, and her 'let-down' reflex is likely to be less efficient.

In spite of these difficulties a number of adoptive mothers have succeeded in breast feeding. Initially they have given the baby both breast milk and formula milk, and as their own supply has increased have reduced the amount of formula feeds, substituting breast feeds. The process may be completed in two or three weeks but may take much longer. Frequent suckling encourages the milk flow; if the baby co-operates it should be put to the breast at about two-hourly intervals.

Three other aids (one human and two inanimate) to help adoptive mothers breast feed are available. The first is a person who is knowledgeable about breast feeding and who will 'mother the mother'. The second is a piece of equipment called a Lact-Aid (Fig. 22): this apparatus delivers milk from a soft plastic container, which the woman secures to her clothing above her breast, through a plastic tube which the baby sucks as he suckles at her nipple. The third is the use of certain medications which cause the secretion of prolactin as already mentioned.

If you adopt a baby and decide that you would like to breast feed him, the message is 'Go on and try', but you will need help from your husband and from a trusted friend who can mother you – and you must not feel guilty or disappointed if you do not succeed.

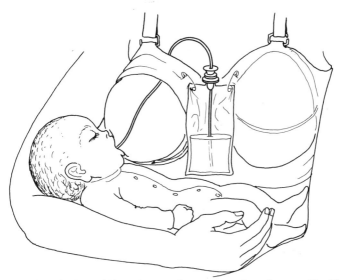

Fig. 22   The Lact-Aid nursing supplementer consists of a resterilizable bag holding 120ml of formula milk or donated human milk, with a plastic tube which the baby sucks as he suckles the nipple

BABY, CHUBBY OR THIN

Is a chubby baby healthier than a thin one?

Custom, relatives, friends, acquaintances, the advertising media and baby health clinic nurses conspire to suggest that chubbiness in babies equates to health. It doesn't, but it will be a long time before mothers accept this. A thin, happy, contented baby is as healthy as a fat, happy, contented baby.

Fat babies are often unhealthy. Usually they have been bottle fed, and often have been given extra semi-solid feeds too early in life or are getting too much salt. Babies do not need solids until they are at least four months old and preferably older. A breast-fed baby cannot get too much salt, but a bottle-fed baby can, if the mother makes up the formula milk incorrectly.

Breast-fed babies grow into all kinds of shapes and sizes. Some are thin, some are fat, some are neither. If your baby is feeding every two, three or four hours, if his nappies are wet, if he has good skin elasticity and clear eyes, he is healthy – so don't worry about his weight.

BIRTH WEIGHT: WHEN REGAINED

How soon after being born will my baby regain his birth weight?

This question correctly supposes that babies lose weight in the first days after birth. This is normal. Some of the weight loss is due to fluid loss, and some because the baby is using up its energy stores pending the time when your milk 'comes in'.

The baby has sufficient fluid and energy stores to cope, and doesn't need any supplements, such as water or glucose water, although these are sometimes given by misguided nurses. The baby only needs to be cuddled and to suckle. Suckling stimulates the prolactin reflex, which encourages milk production and enables the baby to obtain colostrum. Although colostrum provides little fluid or energy it gives the baby protective antibodies and other anti-infection substances.

Your baby can be expected to lose between 6 and 10 per cent of his birth weight before your milk is flowing freely and he starts to gain weight. The amount he loses depends to some extent upon the baby himself, and to some extent on the way he is fed. Babies fed on 'demand' lose less weight and regain their birth weight more rapidly than babies fed three-hourly, who in turn 'perform' better than babies fed four-hourly.

If he is contented and happy, and if his nappy is wet when you change it at each feed, he is doing well. Most babies regain their birth weight in 10 days but some babies take two or three weeks to regain their birth weight. If your baby is breast fed, don't worry and certainly do not give complementary feeds. If you do, the baby will suck you less strongly and your milk supply may be reduced. If you are worried about his slow gain in weight, feed him more often. This will encourage your milk production and your 'let-down' reflex.

A few babies seem contented, suck well but fail to gain weight. If your baby has not regained his birth weight within three weeks it is wise to have him checked by a paediatrician.

BITING AND BABY TEETH

My baby was born with two teeth, is there something wrong – and can I breast feed or will he bite me?

A few babies are born with one or two small front teeth, although teething usually does not occur until the baby is about six months old. The baby who is born with one or two teeth is quite normal, as all the milk teeth are present at birth lying deep in the gums. It is merely that dentition has begun early in these particular babies. No further teeth will erupt until the baby is about six months old.

You can breast feed a baby who has early dentition because his gums are not really used when he feeds. The suction comes from the way the baby squeezes on your nipple with his tongue by pressing it up against his palate.

A few older babies may bite the nipple. Usually the baby is so excited about the feed that he can't wait until the mother's nipple is deep inside his mouth. Some babies 'bite' to see the mother's reaction! Be firm but gentle. Detach him from your breast, tell him you don't like it (he will understand the tone of your voice) and start again.

BRAS AND BREAST FEEDING

Do I need to wear a bra if I decide to breast feed?

Most women in the world who breast feed don't wear a bra. Whether you do or not depends on your own feeling of comfort. During pregnancy your breasts increase in size and become heavier, and in the last weeks you may feel more comfortable if you wear a good uplift bra which has wide straps and well-distributed support. You will find that you need a bra with cups one or two sizes larger than usual. Support for your breasts is thought to help the blood circulation, but there is no real evidence that it does, so if you prefer the freedom of not wearing a bra, it is quite proper to avoid doing so.

When the baby has been born you may choose not to wear a bra, to continue using the bra you bought in late pregnancy, or to purchase a nursing bra. The advantage of the nursing bra is that it opens in the front and you don't have to manipulate your breasts to get them out as you would if you wore an ordinary bra.

There are two kinds of nursing bra. One has a flap for each cup, so that the nipple and areola are easily reached. The second opens down between the cups.

In the first weeks after the baby has been born you may find that milk leaks before (and often between) feeds, due to the strong 'let-down' reflex. Because of this, cotton bras are preferable to nylon bras, and the bra should fit well so that it does not compress your breast. If leaking concerns you, you can tuck a nursing pad of a soft material inside your bra to soak up any leaking milk. You can buy nursing pads at the pharmacy (chemist) or can make them out of old terry towelling nappies. It is wise not to use cotton wool or paper, as they tend to stick to the nipple when they dry. It is also wise to avoid plastic-backed nipple pads as they stop the proper circulation of air around the nipples, which may then become 'soggy' and likely to be damaged when the baby suckles.

Obviously you will need several bras (if you choose to wear them) and changes of clothes, because leaking is common, and babies tend to regurgitate milk, usually when you least expect them to.

You will also have to think of what clothes to wear when you are breast feeding. Today the choice is wide. You will probably find it more convenient to wear blouses, T-shirts or jumpers which can be pulled up, or which open down the front, but you can wear glamorous clothes and still breast feed. Many women are embarrassed about exposing their breasts, and the clothes mentioned make it easy to breast feed with discretion!

BREAST AUGMENTATION AND BREAST FEEDING

Is it possible to breast feed after having a silicone implant to increase the size of the breast?

A woman whose poor breast development causes her to feel socially or sexually inadequate can have the size of her breasts increased by surgery. A carefully chosen silicone implant is introduced to lie behind the breast tissue and in front of the pectoral muscle. The implant consists of a thin silicone sac which is filled with a silicone gel, the amount being decided on by the woman and the plastic surgeon. The implant is introduced either by making a small incision around the lower edge of the areola and 'tunnelling' between the skin and the breast tissue to reach the area behind the breast, or by making a curved incision in the fold below each breast.

As normal breast tissue overlies the implant there is usually no reduction in the sensitivity of the breast or the nipple and the woman has no reduced ability to breast feed.

BREAST CANCER AND PREGNANCY

What is the relationship between breast cancer and pregnancy?

Breast cancer diagnosed when a woman is pregnant is uncommon, fewer than one pregnancy in every 3500 being affected in this way. If a woman who is pregnant is diagnosed as having breast cancer, the emotional shock is considerable and helpful counselling is essential. It is likely that several questions will occur to her and to her family. These include:

- Will the pregnancy increase the spread of the cancer and reduce my chance of cure?
- Will I be able to be treated adequately, when I am pregnant?
- Should I have my pregnancy terminated?
- What should I do about breast feeding?

Pregnancy does not increase the chance of the cancer spreading, but does affect decisions about treatment. The surgical treatment of breast cancer by mastectomy does not affect the fetus, but if it is decided that cytotoxic drugs are required after surgery, these may damage the fetus. For this reason, a full and frank discussion is required between the woman, her husband and her doctor, so that a decision whether or not to terminate the pregnancy can be made. If the use of cytotoxic drugs is not contemplated, the pregnancy can continue, although the parents have the right to seek an abortion if they feel the strain on the mother of having to cope with breast cancer and a baby is too great.

The only prohibition for a pregnant woman who has breast cancer is that she must not breast feed her baby.

Some women who have had breast cancer treated may wish for a pregnancy but are concerned that the pregnancy will affect their chance of survival adversely. Pregnancy does not affect the prognosis, and may be embarked upon if the couple desire this, although they must understand that a woman who has had breast cancer has a greater risk of dying at an earlier age than a woman who has not had the disease.

BREAST CANCER AND LACTATION

Does breast feeding protect a woman against developing breast cancer?

In nations where breast feeding is general and a woman has between three and seven children, breast cancer is less common than in nations where babies are bottle fed. In contrast, in nations where breast feeding is diminishing and families are small, breast cancer seems to be increasing. It would be nice to be able to say that breast feeding protects a woman against breast cancer, but the evidence does not support this: factors such as heredity, obesity and diet may be involved. The matter remains controversial.

BREAST DISEASE AND THE PILL

When I stop breast feeding I intend to take the Pill. If I do, am I more likely to develop breast tumours, particularly breast cancer?

The known fact that oestrogen is a hormone which promotes growth, and the known relationship between oestrogen taken by menopausal women and the subsequent development of cancer of the uterus, has caused anxiety that the Pill (and other forms of hormonal contraception) may increase the chances of a woman developing breast tumours. Recent evidence shows that women who choose the Pill, in preference to other contraceptives, have less breast discomfort and pain in the premenstrual period, and if they have been using the Pill for at least two years are less likely to have painful or tender breasts throughout the menstrual cycle (benign breast disease). Studies in Britain, Sweden and the USA also show that the Pill reduces by half the chance that a woman will develop a benign breast tumour. The relationship between the use of the Pill and the subsequent development of breast cancer has also been investigated. The studies are reassuring, although the proviso has to be made that the interaction between oral contraceptives and other risk factors has not been studied in detail, and there is as yet no prolonged follow-up of women who have used oral contraceptives for long periods. The evidence that oral contraceptives do not add to the risk of a woman developing breast cancer is, first, there has been no increase in the prevalence of the disease since 1950. Second, case control studies have failed to show any increased incidence of breast cancer among oral contraceptive users. In fact, there is the suggestion that oral contraceptives have a beneficial biological effect on the rate of growth of breast cancer.

The answer to the question: Is a woman who chooses the Pill more likely to develop breast disease, including breast cancer? is: No, she is not.

BREAST: EMPTYING AFTER FEED

I have been told I should always empty my breasts by hand-expressing them or using a breast pump after a feed to encourage milk production. Is this true?

This idea was fashionable at one time and was based on the theory that the more the breasts were stimulated, the more efficient was the prolactin reflex. While this is true during the time when lactation is initiated, it is now known that once lactation is established, the baby's suckling creates its own supply and demand situation, and *routine* hand-expression after a feed is no longer advised.

In some circumstances there is a place for hand-expressing milk. Breast feeding is time-demanding and there are occasions when a lactating mother may wish to go out but finds it inconvenient to take the baby with her. She can overcome this problem by hand-expressing after some of the feeds before her excursion and freezing the milk. She should express the milk into a sterile container, cool it in the refrigerator, then pour it into a plastic feeding bottle and freeze it. (Plastic containers and bottles are sterilized in a chemical solution using Milton or Boots tablets.) After the next feed she repeats the process, cooling the expressed milk in the refrigerator and then pouring it on top of the frozen layer of breast milk in the feeding bottle. She continues until the bottle is full.

The frozen milk is thawed by placing the container under running cold water. Once it has liquefied it is warmed to body temperature and given to the baby when it is wanted; but it should probably not be kept for more than 21 days.

If the mother knows of her excursion a day in advance, she does not need to freeze the expressed breast milk. She can collect it after each feed and store it in a domestic refrigerator. It will remain safe for the baby for 24 hours.

BREASTS: EXTRA

I have a small 'extra breast'. Is it likely to enlarge when I become pregnant and particularly when I breast feed?

The breasts, or mammary glands, develop in all species of mammal along a line of tissue in the skin which runs from the armpit along each side of the chest and stomach to the pubic bone or even, in whales and dolphins, down to the vulva, where these species have functioning breasts (Fig. 23).

The number of breasts depends on the number of young normally born to the particular species. Animals which have large litters have several breasts, animals such as primates (monkeys, apes and humans) have small litters and few breasts. Between one and two women in every 100 are born with more than a single pair of breasts, the extra breasts developing along the milk line. As these are inherited, it is usual that some relatives will also have an extra breast. Most accessory breasts consist only of a nipple and have no breast ducts. These are of no importance provided someone explains what has happened.

Occasionally, after puberty, the extra breast develops into a small but obvious breast. This means that ducts and ductules have formed in the tissues and are connected to the nipple. During pregnancy the accessory breast may increase in size and may produce milk during lactation. Some women feed their baby from the accessory breast.

However, most extra breasts consist only of a nipple and only limited development occurs in pregnancy or lactation.

BREASTS: PERSISTENCE OF

The breasts of all other mammals are flat and small except when the animal is lactating. Why do a woman's breasts remain large and conical in shape and protuberant when she is not lactating?

Anthropologists derive a good deal of speculative fun in trying to decide why the human female should have the unique attribute of permanently enlarged breasts from puberty onwards, while those of other female mammals disappear when the animal is not lactating.

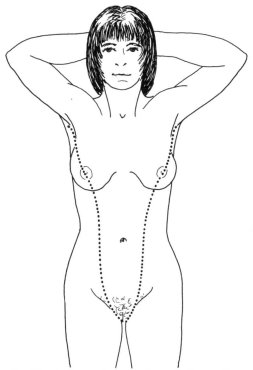

Fig. 23 Accessory breasts along the breast line

One belief is that the human female developed breasts (and a new form of sexuality) when the earliest of man's ancestors stood up and walked upright, at least five million years ago. Before the change to bipedal locomotion occurred, a female mammal signalled to the males in the area that she was biologically ready to become pregnant and was sexually receptive, by developing a coloured swelling of her vulva and by producing vaginal secretions, called pheromones, which attracted any male in the area. She was 'in heat' and accepted any number of males for brief copulations that usually lasted less than 30 seconds. When man's ancestors started to walk upright, the female vulva became largely invisible and ceased to be a sexual attractant. And although human females continued to secrete pheromones, their strength and the ability of the males to scent them diminished.

To replace these sexual attractants and so to enable the race to be perpetuated, over the millennia female Homo, our ancestor, began to develop a new sexual attractant – her breasts. In the upright position the breasts were clearly visible and became sexual signals. But as the size of the breasts did not visibly change when the woman was 'in heat', she had to devise a new method of ensuring that the race would be reproduced. She became sexually responsive and receptive at all times, including the times when she ovulated at about 28-day intervals. The change led to an alteration in sexual behaviour. Other female mammals are only sexually receptive at the time they ovulate, when they copulate briefly with any number of males. Human females, in contrast, tend to form long-lasting relationships; they copulate irrespective of ovulation and each sexual encounter usually lasts longer than 30 seconds!

It may be speculated that the sight of the woman's breasts maintains the man's sexual desire, so that if copulation takes place often it is likely to occur by chance, rather than design, at the time of ovulation and a pregnancy may result.

BREAST FEEDING: CONTRA-INDICATIONS

Are there any contra-indications to breast feeding?

The mother

Apart from active pulmonary tuberculosis, advanced cancer (when the mother is too ill), terminal kidney disease and psychotic mental illness, there are no real contra-indications to breast feeding. Acute illnesses, such as virus influenza, pneumonia and acute kidney infection, are usually over quickly. During the acute infection the milk supply may diminish, and the baby may need complementary feeds. But if the breasts are expressed to remove what milk remains, in most cases the mother will be able to re-establish lactation fully.

The following problems (in alphabetical order) may require discussion before breast feeding is started.

Breast cancer	A family history of breast cancer is not a contra-indication for breast feeding, but a mother who has been treated for breast cancer should not breast feed.
Diabetes	Most diabetic mothers can breast feed quite satisfactorily if they want to. Some diabetic women find that it takes the milk a little longer to 'come in'.
Pulmonary tuberculosis (active)	If the baby is given anti-tuberculosis drugs, the mother may breast feed.

The baby

Mental handicap	Mentally handicapped babies are slow feeders, but if the mother is prepared to breast feed, most babies learn to suck quite quickly.
Inherited metabolic disorders	Babies who have *phenylketonuria* (and some other rare inherited metabolic diseases) should not be breast fed, although human milk contains less of the particular amino acid which causes the disease than cow's milk. These babies require special milk formulas. Phenylketonuria affects only one baby in every 10 000 born.

Galactosaemia is an even rarer inherited disorder and affects one baby in 30 000. The baby has to avoid lactose-containing foods, otherwise vomiting, jaundice, fits and growth retardation may occur. These foods include breast milk and cow's milk, and special formula milks based on soya bean or vegetable oils should be chosen for feeding the baby.

BREAST FEEDING: COSTS OF

Is it cheaper to breast feed than to bottle feed?

During pregnancy, an average, well-nourished woman living in the developed nations will gain about 12.5kg in weight. Between 3 and 4kg of this weight gain is due to the deposition of fat in her body which is laid down mostly before the 30th week of pregnancy. After childbirth, these fat stores are available to release extra energy needed for lactation. They contain about 35 000kcal(146 650kJ) of which about 30 000kcal(125 700kJ) is available for milk production. (The rest is needed to convert the fat into energy.) At its peak the daily energy cost of milk production is about 500kcal(2095kJ) a day. If a mother breast feeds for six months and if she uses the energy stored in her fat, it will provide about 200kcal(838kJ) a day, leaving a deficit of 300kcal(1257kJ) a day. An average woman in the developed nations needs about 2400kcal(10 056kJ) for her daily activities. Most women take in more energy than this, because most eat more food. But if a woman feels it important to obtain the extra 300kcal(1257kJ) she needs for lactation, she can obtain it by eating a rather larger helping at her main meal, or by eating one extra slice of wholemeal bread with butter and cheese, or a large potato with 30g butter and drinking about 100ml of extra milk each day.

The cost of this extra food is about one-quarter of the cost of buying formula-milk feeds for her baby. To the cost of the formula, she has to add the cost of the bottles and teats she uses, the cost of sterilizing them and of replacing them when they break. Breast milk is ready to use, pre-sterilized and the breasts are unlikely to break!

Women in the developing nations, particularly those living in urban slums and in the villages, often eat a diet which provides less than the quantity of energy needed for everyday activities, many obtaining less than 1500kcal(6285kJ) a day. In other words they are hungry and undernourished. During pregnancy, these women are unable to lay down much fat, and many of the poorest women only lay down between 0.5 and 1.0kg.

However, lactating women are more efficient in their absorption of food, and also more efficient in their use of energy, so that many are able to produce milk in spite of a low energy and protein intake. In India, even the poorest women manage to breast feed their babies adequately for six months; but in many countries in Africa and Latin America, solids are given when the baby is two or three months old because the woman believes that she has insufficient milk for its needs. In part she may be right, because she has noticed that its growth rate is faltering and it cries more. To compensate, the mother gives her baby pap or gruel made from local cereals mixed with contaminated water, or if she can afford it buys sweetened condensed milk which she over-dilutes to make it go further. The result is that the baby continues to be hungry and malnourished and at great risk of developing diarrhoeal or respiratory infection. In the Gambia, for instance, in one rural area, half of all babies born had died by the age of five, and by two years of age, two-thirds of those surviving had protein-energy malnutrition.

This appalling situation occurs in many other Third World nations, particularly in remote rural areas. The problem is what can be done? The provision of formula milk for these babies is neither desirable, nor practical. Nor is it sufficient to provide supplementary food for lactating women, as most of the extra energy will first be used to replenish the woman's body fat rather than to help in producing milk.

But if the woman receives food supplements from the beginning of pregnancy so that she is able to lay down fat stores, and continues to receive food supplements while she is breast feeding, she will be able to secrete sufficient milk for the baby's needs, at least for the first six months of its life, and the problem will be overcome. The type of food for the supplements should be chosen from foods usually eaten in the area and should provide between 400kcal(1676kJ) and 800kcal(3532kJ) each day. Educational campaigns to ensure that the mother (rather than her family) eats the food supplements will be needed if the scheme is to succeed.

BREAST FEEDING: DURATION OF A FEED

How long should a feed last?
There is no ideal time. It depends on the baby. Babies vary in the time they take to be satisfied. Some babies seem to prefer to suckle for five to 10 minutes, other babies seem to want to suckle for 40 minutes. The average time a baby seems to prefer is about 15 or 20 minutes. Recent investigations in Oxford have shown that about 50 per cent of the feed from each breast is taken by the baby within the first two minutes, and between 80 and 90 per cent by the end of four minutes. If this research is confirmed it appears that the first five

minutes on each breast provide most of the nutrition and the remaining duration is non-nutritive but may be important for the mother by stimulating the prolactin reflex, and for the baby by providing security, warmth and bonding. In the early part of a feed the baby suckles vigorously, but after five minutes suckling he increases the interval between each burst of suckling. The time it takes to satisfy the baby is no indication of the quality of the mother's breast milk.

BREAST FEEDING: HOW LONG?

For how many months should I breast feed to give my baby the most benefit?

It is generally accepted that for the first four to six months of life, or thereabouts, breast milk provides all the necessary energy and nutrients for normal growth of a baby, and during this period he needs no food other than breast milk. The idea of adding solids to a baby's diet before five months of age, which was fashionable some years ago, has now been shown to be unnecessary and probably unwise.

Sometime between the fourth and the sixth month, a mother may offer her breast-fed baby family food in the form of mashed banana or well-minced or mashed portions of the food eaten by the rest of the family. If the baby isn't interested in the particular food offered, the mother should not persist. She should try again on another day. When the baby is ready, he'll experiment and try the new taste. Babies vary considerably in their food habits. Some gobble up solids at four months; others do not want any food except breast milk until they are six months old or more.

Mothers whose babies are contentedly feeding exclusively on breast milk must beware of becoming anxious or competitive about their baby's progress, for example, when a neighbour boasts that her three-month-old baby is on solids, and thriving! Every baby is an individual. If your baby is thriving he doesn't need solids, and it is bad to give solids before the baby is at least five, and preferably, six months old.

Recently there has been some concern that breast milk provides insufficient food for babies aged between three and six months, particularly if the mother is undernourished. For example, it has been observed that the weight of Gambian babies 'falters' three to six months after birth when compared with the growth rate of British babies. The inference from these studies is that many infants in the developing nations require complementary feeds from three months on if they are to maintain the momentum of their growth. A second inference is that infant foods, especially formula milk, are appropriate in their case, even though most authorities now recommend exclusive breast feeding for the first five or six months of life.

These arguments may not be well founded. For example, an investigation in Western Australia showed that the weight gain of exclusively breast-fed babies, whose mothers were well-nourished middle-class women, also slowed down in the second three months of life. The actual weight gain in this period was very similar to that of breast-fed Australian babies surveyed in 1933 and in 1972–6, of American babies in a 1953 survey, and of babies in 13 developing nations.

This suggests that in the second three months of life the weight gain of well-nourished babies falters, and this is a physiological phenomenon. The reason for the statement that the growth rate of Gambian babies faltered compared with that of British babies was that the weight of the British babies had been taken from a Ministry of Health publication *Standards of Normal Weight in Infancy*. There is evidence that the British babies were not exclusively breast fed, that they may have been overfed with 'solids' and that consequently they were abnormally heavy at the ages of three to six months.

The sensible approach is to breast feed as long as you feel comfortable and your baby is thriving. From between four and six months you may offer him some of the food the family eats, or if you prefer you can give him canned baby foods.

From the time a baby is six months old his chewing mechanisms and digestive system have matured and he will probably want solid foods, which can begin to replace exclusive breast feeding. However, he will still need milk for another six months or, if you feel inclined to continue breast feeding, even longer.

BREAST FEEDING IN PUBLIC

I have been criticized for breast feeding my baby in public. Am I wrong to do this?

It has been said that Anglo-Saxon races are 'mammary-fixated'.

Breasts are extensively used in advertising to stimulate the sales of goods as different as soft drinks and computers. In recent years the taboo about exposed breasts has been much reduced. Magazines openly show breasts with the areolae and nipples prominent. On television and on stage, breasts are exposed. On beaches brief bikini tops, or no top at all, are commonplace and accepted.

At the same time, many mothers are embarrassed about being seen when breast feeding, something which women in the developing world do without embarrassment, although most of them would be embarrassed to wear the scanty clothes favoured in our culture. Recently in Sydney, Australia, a woman who was quietly breast feeding her baby on a bus was told to leave by the conductor. In California, a young married teacher at a college was suspended by the authorities for feeding her four-month-old baby on campus.

Changes are occurring and breast feeding in company is more common today. You should do what you feel is most comfortable for you. If you want to feed only in private, in seclusion, do that. If you happen to be in company when your baby wants to be fed, feed him. You can be quite discreet when feeding, if you feel you may embarrass the other people around you. The important thing is to be able to feed your baby when he wants to be fed, not to wait because other people might object.

BREAST INFECTIONS

What about breast infection?

Breast infections usually start because bacteria enter through a fissure or crack in the nipple. Most fissures begin near the base of the nipple. They can be excruciatingly painful and many mothers stop breast feeding because of them.

Fissures and cracks can be prevented by taking the measures outlined on page 142. If a crack or fissure appears a mother should take all the steps listed for treating sore nipples. But if the nipple does not heal within three or four days she will probably wish to take her baby off the breast and give him expressed breast milk for a few days, either hand-expressing or using a breast pump.

When the crack has healed she can start feeding again, once or twice a day at first, continuing to express for the other feeds, gradually building up until she is fully breast feeding once again.

In a few cases, the condition, instead of resolving, gets worse and breast infection develops.

Infection of a Montgomery follicle

A few nursing mothers develop a small area of superficial infection in the second or third week after birth, in or near a Montgomery follicle in the areola. A small lump appears, developing slowly. The mother feels well, and feeding is not disturbed. The lump contains pus, so that antibiotics should be given. If these do not clear up the lump within 24 hours it will need to be incised.

Intramammary mastitis, 'blocked ducts'

Most paediatric textbooks suggest that a main duct leading from a lobe may become blocked due to pressure from a badly fitting bra or because the breast becomes so engorged with milk that the swollen alveoli press on and block the duct. The result is that when the baby sucks, more milk is produced, but it is unable to reach the nipple because the main duct is blocked. The pressure behind the block increases and eventually some of the alveoli burst, letting milk escape into the tissues surrounding the 'milk tree'. Fluid also escapes from the distended veins.

The result is a tender area in the breast, with a red area of skin over it. If the milk in the tissues of the breast becomes infected, a tense, tender area results, the woman develops a raised temperature and feels ill with generalized aches.

Another explanation is that 'blocked duct' or 'caked breast' is due to infection entering through an abrasion or crack in a nipple. The bacteria are carried by the lymphatic vessels of the breast and infect the tissues between the ducts, causing a local area of cellulitis. As the tissues become swollen the main duct is to some extent obstructed.

If a mother thinks she has a blocked duct she should take action to prevent it getting worse. She should feed her baby often and empty her breasts after each feed. If the breasts are still lumpy after this she should try to get the baby to take extra feeds. She may also try hot and cold towels on her breasts every hour or so, and check that her bra fits properly and is not too tight. Before and after each feed she should massage the breast gently towards the nipple, starting from the lump.

It must be said that a good deal of controversy exists about breast massage as a means of relieving a blocked duct. Some doctors recommend that the breast is massaged gently; others believe that massage does not help.

If a mother decides to try hand-massage she must be gentle and avoid hurting herself. In this situation a vibrator may be preferable (see p. 108). But if the tender lump persists for 24 hours or if the mother develops a temperature, she should visit her doctor as she may have developed mastitis.

Mastitis

Between 2 and 5 per cent of lactating women develop an in-flammation of a segment of the breast tissue. This is caused by in-fection entering through a cracked nipple. Infection is usually the result of poor nursing techniques. If the breast is engorged and the baby is unable to get the nipple and areola well into his mouth, he will chew on the nipple and damage it. If a blocked duct is not treated adequately and complete drainage of the breasts is not achieved after feeding, the milk may stagnate – a perfect site for infection.

At first the infection develops in the tissues between the lobules, and a *segment* of the breast becomes red, tender and throbs. Because the infection is a cellulitis there is no pus in the milk ducts.

There are two principles in treating mastitis in breast-feeding mothers. The first is to empty the breast regularly. The second is to kill the infecting bacteria. In the early stages of mastitis, the mother should nurse frequently to empty the breast. She won't infect her baby. Her doctor will prescribe large doses of an antibiotic; usually a penicillin is chosen and at present flucloxacillin (Floxapen) is preferred, as it attacks bacteria which are resistant to ordinary penicillin. The antibiotic should be given as early as possible, because if mastitis is left untreated for more than 24 hours a breast abscess is likely to occur.

Feeding may be painful and the mother may wish to take analgesics about half an hour before putting the baby to the breast.

Breast abscess

If an abscess forms, as it does in about 7 per cent of women who develop mastitis, the mother feels ill and may be feverish. Her breast will be painful, red and tender. If this happens, the mother should

not feed on the affected breast until it has healed, but can continue
to feed on the other breast.

BREAST MILK: ANTI-INFECTIVE PROPERTIES

*Breast milk is said to contain substances which protect the baby against
infections, particularly gastro-enteritis and chest infections. Is this true?*
Investigations in many countries, both developed countries like
Sweden and Britain, and developing countries like Thailand, Guata-
mala and Jamaica show that bottle-fed babies are between three and
12 times more likely to develop infective diarrhoea, viral chest infections and meningitis, compared with breast-fed babies. It was
thought that the difference was due to poor hygiene in the preparation of the formula (dirty bottle and teat, infected milk or water)
and to infections of other children in the family. These two factors
play a major part, but the protective anti-infective effect of breast
milk itself is also important.

Breast milk contains at least four anti-infective protective substances which are largely absent from cow's milk. These are secretory
immunoglobulin A, lactoferrin, lysosyme and maternal macrophages (killer cells).

Secretory immunoglobulin A (sIgA) is a protective substance secreted
by the lining cells of the intestine. It makes an 'antiseptic intestinal
paint' which prevents infection entering the cells unless the numbers
of bacteria are great. The intestinal cells of babies in the first six to
12 weeks of life are unable to make secretory IgA. These young
babies are consequently at greater risk of developing intestinal infections. Fortunately, breast milk contains secretory IgA, which is made
in the breast milk-producing cells. The earliest milk, colostrum, contains the greatest amounts of secretory IgA (with 10 to 100 times the
amount found in the blood), and later mature milk also has high
levels. Until the baby is able to make his own secretory IgA, breast
milk, by providing sIgA, gives him protection; and even after he is
able to make his own secretory IgA, breast milk sIgA adds to the
amount available.

The second protective substance in breast milk is called *lactoferrin*.
This substance prevents bacteria from multiplying in the baby's intestines. It works in conjunction with secretory IgA, each enhancing
the anti-infective activity of the other. Cow's milk contains very little
lactoferrin compared to human milk.

The third anti-infective substance is called *lysosyme*. It is found in concentrations in breast milk up to 5000 times that found in cow's milk. It prevents infective bacteria from multiplying in the baby's intestines, and may perhaps kill various viruses.

The fourth anti-infective substances are maternal white blood cells which get into the milk from the mother's blood, and then into the baby's intestines. The cells, called *macrophages*, search out and kill bacteria which manage to get into the body. When they are absorbed into the baby's body with the other constituents of milk, they retain their ability to kill bacteria. They also synthesize secretory IgA and add this to the baby's supply. The cells of course are absent from cow's milk.

Breast milk, in addition to providing the most appropriate mixture of nutrients for a human baby, also makes available a subtle, complex, effective and specially tailored system of no-cost immunization and prophylaxis against many infections. It has been rightly called a 'potent medicine'.

BREAST MILK: APPEARANCE

I have noticed since I expressed my breast milk that it is bluish in colour and thin. It isn't creamy and yellowish-white like cow's milk. Does this mean it is less nutritious than cow's milk?

The normal colour of human milk is a bluish-white and it is thin in texture. The colour and texture do not tell you about its food value. Human bluish-white milk is more nutritious for the baby than any of the modified cow's milk formula milks available, which look thick and creamy when they have been made up.

BREAST-MILK BANKS

What is the current opinion about providing donor breast milk for small preterm babies?

Human milk is the most appropriate, nutritionally balanced food for human babies; it does not cause allergies and it provides anti-infective substances; for these reasons it has been suggested that breast milk should be made available for feeding preterm babies until the baby's mother is able to start and continue lactating. This process may be delayed, as many mothers of preterm babies are under considerable stress in the early weeks of the baby's life and may be unable to produce sufficient milk for the preterm baby. Human-milk banks have been established in some hospitals to provide milk donated by other breast-feeding mothers, and this milk is available not only for the preterm babies but for other sick infants. The donated milk is hand-expressed or is in the form of 'drip milk', which is the milk that drips from the other breast during feeding. The milk is collected, pooled, pasteurized and frozen. Two major problems regarding donor milk have surfaced. The first is that the donated milk (especially drip milk) may lack sufficient energy, fat, calcium and sodium to meet the particular nutritional needs of a preterm baby. The second problem is that pasteurization effectively eliminates the anti-infective agents in human milk. It could be argued that *freshly* expressed donor breast milk would overcome the second problem. However such milk invariably contains large numbers of bacteria and viruses. These micro-organisms may infect the fragile preterm baby, leading to serious illness. As well as this, human breast-milk banks are expensive, labour intensive and require careful 'quality control' so that the potential hazard of infecting the baby with contaminated milk is reduced.

For these reasons, the place of breast-milk banks is still being researched, and most paediatricians prefer to feed small preterm babies (weighing 1500g or less) with formula milk, changing to the mother's freshly expressed breast milk when the baby weighs more than 1500g, and to breast feeding when the baby is able to suckle.

BREAST LUMPS AND LUMPINESS

I have heard that a woman who breast feeds is more likely to develop breast lumps, or something called fibrocystic disease. Is this true?

Two main kinds of breast lump (apart from cancer) are found in a woman's breasts. The first is more common in women under the age of 30 and is called a fibro-adenoma. The woman notices a single smooth lump in the breast either by chance or because she examines her breasts regularly. The lump seems to move under her fingers, which has led to it being called rather quaintly a 'breast mouse'. It is firm and painless. Investigations, which may include a biopsy of the lump, show that it is not a cancer, but its removal by surgery is usually recommended as the fibro-adenoma often continues to grow. The operation is a minor one and does not even require the woman to stay in hospital. It can be done under local anaesthesia if the woman prefers it.

After the age of 30, the second form of lumpy breasts becomes more common. It is an exaggeration, throughout most of the menstrual cycle, of the premenstrual breast lumpiness which appears in the 10 days before menstruation and disappears when menstruation starts. When the lumpiness and breast discomfort persist through most of the menstrual cycle, the condition is called benign mammary dysplasia or benign breast disease.

In the past, benign mammary dysplasia was given a variety of sinister-sounding names. These included chronic mastitis, chronic cystic mastitis, fibrocystic disease, fibro-adenosis and blue-domed cyst disease. It is now know that the condition does not lead to cancer and it has been given its new name to emphasize that it is benign.

Benign mammary dysplasia is believed to be due to excessive sensitivity of the breast to the normal circulating sex hormones. The hormones lead to an overgrowth and dilation of the ducts in the lactiferous (milk) tree which make the breasts feel lumpy. In some cases the cells which line the ducts start growing inwards so that the duct becomes blocked. If this happens the duct behind the block may dilate and small cysts may form. Sometimes one of the cysts becomes quite big, when it is called a blue-domed cyst from its appearance at surgery.

Both breasts, or only one, may feel lumpy, usually in the upper and outer part. If a woman examines her breasts she will notice that the breast tissues are thickened, with irregular lumpy areas which tend to merge, almost imperceptibly, with normal tissue. Occasionally she may feel a small firm area among the lumps.

A doctor should be consulted, who will palpate the breasts to determine the exact position and size of the lumpy area. He may suggest further investigations by ultrasound or mammography. If a cyst is found he may suggest a *needle aspiration*. A narrow needle is inserted through the breast tissues into the lump, and its contents are aspirated using a syringe. If the lump is a cyst it disappears when it is aspirated. On the other hand, a lump which does not disappear has to be investigated further, usually by removing it from the breast. The operation is a minor one, and the woman does not usually need to remain in hospital for more than a few hours. The doctor makes a small curved incision along one of the tension lines of the breast and dissects carefully until he reaches the lump, which he then excises. Healing is quick and the scar almost invisible if the incision has been made along the tension line. The excised lump is examined in a laboratory to make sure that it is not a breast cancer. Treatment is similar to that suggested for premenstrual breast pain (see below).

It is not true that women who breast feed develop a fibro-adenoma or benign disease more frequently than childless women or those who choose not to breast feed. In fact breast feeding seems to protect women from developing these two breast conditions.

BREASTS: PREMENSTRUAL PAIN

Before I became pregnant I had severe breast pain in the week before my menstrual period. Is this likely to occur when I stop breast feeding?

When a woman ceases to lactate and ovulation starts again, premenstrual breast tenderness and pain are likely to recur. During the menstrual cycle most women's breasts increase in size – starting at mid-cycle, and reaching a maximum by the first day of menstruation. The increased breast size is not noticed by many women, but some women complain of breast tenderness or breast pain during the seven to 10 days before menstruation. These women observe that if they palpate their breasts in the premenstrual period they can detect lumpy or knobby areas usually in the upper, outer portion, rather as if 'someone had put tangles of thick string' in their breast tissues. Until recently doctors believed that women who complained of cyclical breast pain were neurotic, but recent research indicates that the condition may be due to an imbalance of the female sex hormones oestrogen and progesterone, or to an abnormal sensitivity to the hormone prolactin. In some women this imbalance or abnormal sensitivity may be triggered by emotional problems.

On the whole treatment has been, and is, unsatisfactory. A woman should seek an explanation of her problem from a doctor who is prepared to listen and discuss it. Some doctors prescribe diuretics, although the evidence is not strong that quantities of fluid are retained in the breast tissues. Other doctors try to correct the hormone imbalance (if it exists) by giving gestagen hormone tablets or danazol, a drug which counters the actions of the sex hormones on the breast. Perhaps the most hopeful treatment for severe cyclical breast pain is to use the anti-prolactin drug bromocriptine.

BREAST PUMPS

Breast pumps are being advertised increasingly, should I buy one?

Although most women have all the equipment needed for nursing a baby, circumstances may arise when breast expression is needed. For example, a woman who is breast feeding may have to interrupt it temporarily if she or her baby has to be admitted to hospital, as many institutions object to both being admitted. Some mothers may occasionally wish to go out leaving the baby at home, but also wish him to have a feed of breast milk. A mother returning to paid employment may wish to continue breast feeding. There is also the problem of the small preterm baby who has to remain in hospital for a fairly long period after the mother has returned home.

In many cases hand-expression will provide all the milk needed, and hospitals caring for preterm babies may provide the mother with an electric breast pump, the Egnell Pump, which is efficient and can be sterilized easily. However, many women may wish to buy a breast pump, arguing that it is more convenient, and that it avoids even the remote chance of introducing infection, which might occur if several women used the same breast pump.

In America, business has noticed the trend to breast feeding and an industry has arisen in manufacturing personal breast pumps. Some of these are well-made and easily sterilized and maintained, others are less efficient. In the USA, appropriate choices might be the Loyd-B-Pump, the Kaneson Expressing and Feeding Bottle (Fig.24) (which is recommended for women whose babies have a cleft palate) and the Evenflo Pump Kit. None of these requires an electric power source, each one is easily portable and all have good instructions. A novel kind of pump has been developed in Australia. Called the Ellis Pump, it is water powered and connects with a household tap. It is cheap and easily maintained. It is suitable for expressing breast milk for a preterm baby who is not strong enough to feed, or who needs feeds when the mother is not available. It can also be used to treat severe engorgement or to relieve a 'blocked duct'.

Most women do not need to buy a breast pump, and if problems arise are able to hire a pump should this be needed.

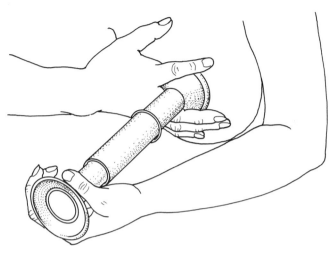

Fig. 24   The Kaneson hand pump

BREAST SELF-EXAMINATION

When I cease to breast feed and my breasts return to normal is it wise to examine them regularly?

It has been shown that most cases of breast cancer are discovered accidentally when a woman finds a lump in her breast. Because breast cancer is more likely to be cured when detected early, many doctors recommend that a woman should examine her breasts each month in the week after menstruation to find out if a lump is present. If she detects a lump, investigations are required, although four out of five lumps prove *not* to be due to cancer – which is reassuring. When a woman stops breast feeding she may wish to begin breast self-examination, because she has become accustomed to touching her breasts when lactating and she is able to palpate them comfortably.

The simplest way for a woman to examine her breasts is outlined below.

Before you have a bath or shower, stand in front of a mirror, put your hands on your sides and look at your breasts. When you are in the bath or under the shower and your skin is wet and soapy, examine your breasts by feeling them gently on each part. If you detect a lump (or an area in your breast which causes you concern), you should make an appointment to see your doctor so that the lump can be investigated further.

A more complicated but good method is that recommended by several cancer societies (Fig. 25). The examination should be done in sequence:

● Stand in front of a mirror, put your hands by your sides and look at your breasts. Then raise your hands above your head and look again. Now put your hands on your hips, press firmly, elbows forward (which puts the pectoral muscles on a stretch) and look again. You are looking at your breasts to see if the shape of either has changed since your last self-examination; if any part of the skin is puckered; if there is a bulge or a flattened area in either breast; or if either nipple has been drawn into the breast tissue.

● Next, lie down on a bed, a couch or, if you prefer, in your bath. If you lie on your bed, put a pillow under the shoulder on the side of the breast you are going to examine. You will find it easier to examine your breast if the skin is wet and, if possible, soapy.

As you examine each breast, raise the arm on that side above your head. The pillow under your shoulder, and the raised arm spread the breast tissue more evenly over your ribcage and make the palpation easier. Palpation means to examine gently, using the flat of your first three fingers held together. Feel each breast gently and systematically with the flat of the fingers of the opposite hand. Start at the upper, outer part of the breast and work your way round, moving your fingers in small circles until you have palpated the entire breast. Finally return to the upper area, between your nipple and armpit, and palpate it again, as this is where most lumps will be found. When you have examined one breast, repeat the same procedure on the other.

A woman who is aged 35 or more, should also have an annual breast examination made by a doctor and, when appropriate, mammography (a special x-ray picture of each breast) should be included in the examination.

LOOKING

FEELING

Fig. 25 *Breast self-examination. (1) Look in the mirror; (2) Stretch arms above the head; (3) Place hands on hips and push inwards to the hips; (4) Lying down, head on pillow and a pillow under the shoulder of the side to be palpated, feel the breast with the flat of the first three fingers; (5, 6, 7) Feeling the breast starting from the nipple and moving outward around the breast; (8) Feeling the outer part of the breast particularly; (9) Feeling the tail of the breast which extends towards the armpit*

BREAST SIZE AND LACTATION

I have very small breasts; am I less likely to be able to breast feed my baby than a woman with big breasts?

The size of a woman's breasts depends more on the amount of fat deposited between the branches and tufts of the 'milk tree' than on the development of the milk-secreting alveoli. During pregnancy the alveoli and the ducts increase in number and in size, but the amount of fat laid down may not increase so much. Most pregnant women's breasts reach their maximum size by 20 weeks and there is no relationship between their size before pregnancy and the amount of enlargement during pregnancy. It follows that the size of a woman's breasts before pregnancy or at childbirth bears no relationship to the amount of milk she can produce or to the efficiency of the 'let-down' reflex. Breast size is not related to milk yield. A woman with small breasts can feed her baby as successfully as a woman with large breasts.

BURPING

Do babies need burping or 'winding'?

Until recently, most mothers in the industrialized countries were taught that unless they burped (winded) their baby during and after a feed, he would not settle and would develop colic (Fig. 26). Recently the need to burp all babies routinely has been questioned, as it has been observed that every baby swallows some air during a feed (just as every adult does). The amount of air swallowed depends on how easily the milk flows. If the flow of milk is slow, more air is swallowed than if it is fast. Some of the air may come up as a burp, the rest passes into the intestines, to emerge later with a noise! It has also been observed that in the developing nations, where babies are fed on demand and often carried in a sling, mothers do not find it necessary to burp their babies, and are amused watching European mothers going through the ritual.

In order to find out more, the author asked the views of 100 women about burping. Twenty per cent regularly burped their baby and believed that burping was needed to settle him. One mother wrote: 'We started to burp Christopher, and those bubbles of air – once brought up – certainly made a world of difference to him. He

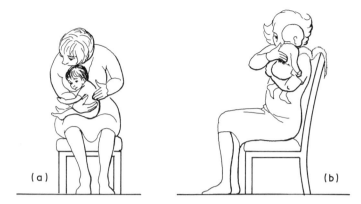

Fig. 26   'Burping'. Bringing up wind after a feed by rubbing or patting the baby's back either while he is sitting on the mother's lap (a) or resting on her shoulder (b)

settled more easily and was not as restless.' Another mother regularly burped her baby because: 'Burping does help a baby settle in many cases. Not because the baby has pain, but because the stroking and close physical contact involved relaxes the child and a more relaxed child is ready for sleep.'

Twenty-five per cent of mothers did not find it necessary to burp their baby, although some had burped previous babies. A mother wrote: 'I burped my first baby because when I trained as a nurse I was taught that babies had wind and so must be burped. Also my mother and mother-in-law expected me to do it. That poor little boy was dosed on gripe-water, patted on the back, and so on until he burped. He cried a lot and I presumed he had wind. . . . My second didn't have wind. The reason he didn't was because I chose to ignore the traditional thing of thumping his back until he burped. . . . When I look back I realize why my first baby cried so much. It wasn't wind, it was an accumulation of circumstances. He was fed strictly to a time schedule in hospital; I was tense and uptight.' Another mother wrote: 'In the first weeks with my first child, I listened to hospital staff, friends and family about the necessity to burp her. She was totally unimpressed at being disturbed during a feed so I discontinued. If she wants to burp she will do so when moved from one breast to another.'

The majority of women – 54 per cent – did what might be called a modified burping: they sat the baby upright after feeding from the first breast, talked and played with the baby for a while, and if a 'burp' came up that was fine, but if it didn't they fed the baby at the second breast. A mother wrote: 'I do burp my baby. . . . By burping I do not mean the ritualistic back pounding and rubbing that I have seen so many mothers perform, but simply a rest from drinking during which time he invariably burped.'

Some of the women who used the modified burping technique believed that tenseness in the mother might affect the baby. For example: 'I do believe that babies get wind problems. However, I think that the best way to alleviate the problem is not by slapping, patting or thumping. I think relaxation is very important both for mother and baby. I used to hold her upright keeping body contact, cuddle and talk with her after each feed and sometimes she would burp, sometimes she wouldn't. I don't think it made a great deal of difference to her ability to settle down. If she hadn't burped after about five minutes or so, I didn't make an issue of it, but would settle her and she would sleep.'

The experiences of these mothers suggest that most women 'burp' their baby because their relatives or their medical attendants have taught them that burping is necessary to settle him. In addition, it appears that babies fed on 'demand' and carried in a sling settle more easily. A mother suggested that 'perhaps in our society the baby is missing the constant movement and warmth he gets in societies where the baby is carried.' Another mother confirmed this: 'I worked in Papua-New Guinea for two years. I never saw a Papuan mother intentionally burp a baby. . . . Despite my Papuan experience I am burping my babies. Why? I'm not sure. I suspect it helps me feel better if I think I'm doing something for my crying or unsettled baby. Certainly rhythmic patting or rocking seems to soothe the baby and often produces a burp. I guess the Papuan women were achieving the same thing.'

In this rather confusing situation the advice from a mother of two, who is also a counsellor for the Nursing Mothers' Association of Australia, is perhaps the most appropriate: 'My plea is twofold. First try not burping and see if your baby is happy. Second, if he needs to be burped, be gentle. How would you like to be hit between the shoulder blades between hors-d'oeuvre and entrée, soup and main course? Poor little babies!'

BURPING: MEDICINES FOR

Do any medicines help a baby to bring up wind and relieve his colic?

Most babies who are fed on demand, cuddled and carried a good deal seem not to need 'winding'. However, some babies do not settle easily unless they are burped, and mothers often enquire if any medicine will help the baby bring up wind. Three main groups of medicines are available – gripe-water, dicyclomine (Merbentyl) and dicyclomine with simethicone (Infacol). In a study made recently, most women found gripe-water useless, only half of those who used Merbentyl found that it helped, and only a third of those who used Infacol said it enabled the baby to burp.

The most likely reason for the poor success rate of all the medications is that 'wind' is more often due to crying than crying is due to wind. Most babies need to be cuddled and talked to, rather than fed medicines and put down.

CAESAREAN SECTION AND BREAST FEEDING

I am to have a caesarean section, can I breast feed?

Modern surgical technique and good anaesthesia (especially epidural anaesthesia) have made caesarean section a much less formidable operation than it was in the past. Obviously any abdominal operation is uncomfortable, but stitches to repair an episiotomy may also be uncomfortable.

It is now usual to let the mother hold and cuddle her baby as soon as she feels ready to do so after a caesarean section. If the baby has had to be put in the intensive-care nursery, the mother is taken in a wheelchair to see and to touch him as soon as she feels ready. A mother whose baby has been born by caesarean section can breast feed. She needs more help and encouragement. Because of the operation she may have to try several positions to find the one which is most comfortable for her to breast feed.

In fact, it is usually more comfortable to breast feed than to hand-express the milk, or to suppress lactation with drugs. There is no truth in the belief that after a caesarean section it takes longer for the milk to 'come in'.

CLEFT PALATE

Can a baby with a cleft palate be fed at the breast?

A cleft palate varies considerably in severity. In some babies, the cleft only involves the soft palate at the back of the mouth. In some, the cleft involves the hard palate as well.

Most paediatricians now begin to treat the severe clefts much earlier than in the past. Soon after birth the baby is fitted with a plate in the roof of his mouth. The purpose is to make sure that the two halves of his palate grow equally and become equal size. As he grows, new plates are fitted, and once the two sides are of equal size, the cleft is repaired surgically. If the two sides are of equal size when the baby is examined soon after birth, the plates are not needed and the cleft is repaired at 14 to 18 months of age.

It is worth trying to breast feed, as some babies manage quite well, although feeding takes longer than usual. Feeding with a bottle or from a spoon will also take longer than usual

COELIAC DISEASE

Is it true that coeliac disease is prevented if the baby is breast fed?

There is some recent evidence that this is so. It has been noted recently that in Yorkshire coeliac disease is becoming less common. Dr Littlewood and his colleagues suggest that coeliac disease may be initiated by an attack of gastro-enteritis, which in turn may lead to cow's milk allergy. This causes further damage to the lining of the intestine, to lactose intolerance and to the development of coeliac disease. Dr Littlewood suggests that the falling incidence in coeliac disease may be related to the increasing prevalence of breast feeding and the consequent reduction in gastro-enteritis, and to the delay in introducing solids.

COLIC: 'THREE-MONTH COLIC'

What is the three-month colic?

A considerable number of babies have periods of time when, for no apparent reason, they draw their legs up and scream. Often the baby becomes red in the face, passes wind out of his bottom and seems inconsolable. These episodes are more common in the first three months of life and have been said to be due to 'the three-month colic'. This term was introduced into medical literature to hide the doctor's ignorance of the true cause of the crying. The idea that the crying was due to colic was reinforced by the fact that if the baby was picked up, cuddled, consoled and pacified by its mother he usually stopped crying.

The episodes of screaming frequently take place in the evening, and distress the mother (and her partner). Although doctors do not really know the cause, they believe that certain things 'trigger' the screaming fit. Some of these are anxiety, boredom, hunger, allergies, reflux and perhaps 'wind'.

ANXIETY: Even tiny babies notice what goes on. If the mother is harassed, trying to prepare food or make the house tidy, and is rushing around, the baby may sense that he is being neglected, become anxious and start to scream. This, in turn, makes the mother more anxious, less sure of her ability to cope with her baby and perhaps resentful and frightened of him. Her anxiety is perceived by the baby who becomes more anxious. The anxiety of both mother and baby will be reduced if she picks her baby up, cuddles him and reassures him that he is loved and protected. If she is too tense, she may find it helpful to play with him in the bath, or to ask a relative or a friend to look after him while she calms down. Some couples find that the baby settles if they take him for a drive in their car.

BOREDOM: On the other hand, the baby may be bored or lonely and want attention. It is a fallacy to believe that small babies are inert, insensitive objects that only need to be fed and changed. If the baby has slept for most of the day he may want to play. There are two ways of dealing with this problem. The first is to try and get the baby to stay awake during part of the day. The second is to carry him around in a baby-sling or *mei-tai* for most of the time you are doing the housework.

HUNGER: Some babies cry because they are hungry, so that if the baby continues to scream, in spite of being cuddled, he may stop if he can suck at your breast. Even if he doesn't want food he obtains the warmth and security of your comforting body.

ALLERGIES: Colic is a well-known symptom of allergy to cow's milk protein among bottle-fed babies. Recently it has been found that a few breast-fed babies may develop colic, caused by cow's milk proteins transmitted from the mother by her breast milk. This is more likely to occur if the mother herself has asthma or some other allergy. The treatment is for the mother to avoid drinking cow's milk and eating foods prepared from cow's milk, such as cheese, yoghurt and milk chocolate. If the baby's colic ceases within two or three days of changing the diet, the diagnosis has been established.

REFLUX: Some babies may cry because some of the milk, together with acid stomach contents, leaks upwards into the lowest part of the oesophagus (the food pipe from the mouth to the stomach), where it causes irritation. In adults a similar reflux occurs causing heartburn.

WIND: Many mothers believe that the cause of the baby's screaming is due to wind. If the mother thinks this she may wish to burp her baby but mustn't expect that it will necessarily stop his colic. Screaming babies often 'pass wind' from their gut, because there is always air in the gut, and screaming builds up the abdominal pressure, so the air is forced explosively out of his anus. What is not explained if wind is the cause, is why a baby only screams at certain times of the day: he has wind in his intestines at all times. The explanation does not seem logical!

It can be seen that colic does not have a single cause, and it is unlikely that a major cause is 'wind'. This is the reason why the medications often prescribed are often ineffective.

A mother whose baby has colic needs to be reassured as much as her baby needs to be cuddled. A screaming baby does not mean that the mother is a 'poor' mother. Her partner can help by cuddling and playing with the baby while she does other things. Alternatively he can prepare the food while she lets her baby suckle at her breast. There is no perfect solution, each mother will find the one which works best for her. Occasionally a mild sedative may be prescribed by a doctor for either one of the pair – in honesty, though, the use of sedatives is guesswork, because doctors don't really know why some babies have the screaming episodes which they call 'colic'.

In countries where babies are almost constantly cuddled and

carried around, such as China, India and Indonesia, colic is said to be almost unknown. Perhaps the explanation of colic lies in this finding. Human babies need to be fed frequently, carried most of the time and cuddled often. Perhaps colic is a sign of the baby's anxiety, unhappiness or boredom and not a distinct medical disease.

COLOSTRUM

What is colostrum; does it have any value?

In the second half of pregnancy, colostrum, which is a thick lemon-yellow liquid, begins to be secreted in the breasts. It may leak from the nipples, or may be expressed if a woman massages her breasts. If colostrum leaks it may make the delicate skin of the areola moist and chafed. To prevent this happening, a woman should put a small pad over her nipple to absorb the moisture and may decide to apply some anhydrous lanolin to protect the skin.

Colostrum is also secreted in the first three to five days after the birth of the baby. It is replaced first by transitional milk, the composition of which resembles mature milk; and then from about the 10th to the 15th day mature milk alone is secreted.

Compared with mature milk, colostrum contains less fat, less milk sugar, more protein, and has a high level of anti-infective substances. This suggests that the function of colostrum is to protect the newborn baby from infection; and it may be a laxative, which helps the baby clear its bowels of the green contents (meconium) which have been accumulating in late pregnancy.

COMPLEMENTARY FEEDING

What is complementary feeding?

Complementary feeds are given after the baby has been breast fed, if he is still hungry, to *complement* the amount of milk he obtained. Complementary feeds should not be given while your milk is 'coming in' as they reduce the baby's desire to suck at your breast. This, in turn, reduces the strength of your prolactin reflex and 'let-down' reflex and makes the establishment of breast feeding less certain.

Once breast feeding is established there will be times when you wonder if the baby is really getting enough milk or if he needs more than you can give him from your breasts.

Look at your baby! If he wets seven or eight nappies a day, opens his bowels, and is contented, with an elastic skin and bright eyes, he is getting enough, even though at times he doesn't put on weight. Breast-fed babies do not always gain the steady 125–175g(4–7oz) a week the books say they should. Babies are individuals. Some weeks they will gain more than the 'recommended' amount, some weeks they will gain less, but *on average* they gain between 400–500g (about 1lb) a month.

Look at yourself! Is the quantity of milk you make really low? Even if it is low, you can improve it, and avoid the time and trouble needed to prepare the complementary feed, to feed your baby and to clean up the bottles. Remember, breast milk increases if you are confident.

- Feed your baby more often. The more times he suckles, the more milk you make: a sort of 'demand and supply' situation. Don't cut out night feeds, in fact give an extra night feed if your baby cries.

- Be relaxed, and ignore the conflicting advice friends and health professionals tend to give. If you become concerned about your ability to feed you will suppress your 'let-down' reflex, and your milk supply will fall. During the feed have a drink, or relax by watching the TV or reading, as well as looking at your baby.

- Remember you need time for yourself. Time to relax! Forget the dusting, the unmade beds, the dishes in the sink! You are a mother, and only you can breast feed your baby. The baby's father can't, but he can dust, make beds, wash dishes and do the shopping.

- If your baby still seems hungry after all this, you may have to give him a complementary feed of 'modified' or 'adapted' cow's milk, given at the end of a breast feed. He can be offered about 60ml(2oz), and if he takes it all he may need more another time. If your baby co-operates he should take the complementary feed from a spoon, as some babies tend to prefer a bottle to the breast. But if he splutters and hates it, give him a bottle.

- After you have changed his nappy and put him to bed, express your breasts into a cup (which you have scalded). If there is a good deal of milk left in your breasts you are making enough milk and the baby can be given it if he is hungry after his next feed.

Often the early evening feeds produce the smallest amount of milk, and after these feeds a complementary feed may be needed. But most mothers will find that complementary feeds are not needed if they stimulate their own milk supply by frequent breast feeding, and are confident about their ability to breast feed.

CONSTIPATION

My baby only passes a motion on alternate days. The stool is soft and the baby is healthy, but I am worried about constipation.

Babies, like adults, vary in the frequency with which they open their bowels. Although most breast-fed babies pass a soft motion two or three times a day, some healthy and contented babies may only open their bowels every second day, or even only once a week. Provided the stool is soft when it is passed, it is quite normal. The baby is not constipated. A constipated stool is hard and the baby has to strain to pass it. Constipated stools are unusual in breast-fed babies. Constipation may occur if the baby is underfed or does not absorb enough water.

Mothers should remember that constipation does not induce general ill-health. It does not cause bad breath, a furred tongue, or bad temper. Constipation produces local abdominal discomfort or, if the faeces are like hard nuggets, may cause pain in the rectum when the baby tries to empty its bowels.

CONTRACEPTION AND BREAST FEEDING

Will lactation protect me against an unwanted pregnancy?

Lactation does not *completely* protect a woman against an unwanted pregnancy, although ovulation is unusual in the first 20 weeks after childbirth. Even during these weeks, between 5 and 15 per cent of women ovulate and become pregnant without having had a menstrual period.

Lactation delays the return of ovulation by the action of prolactin.

Prolactin reduces the release of the pituitary hormones (the gonado-trophins) which stimulate the ovary and may act in the ovary itself, inhibiting growth of the egg-follicles. The more suckling that takes place in each 24-hour period, the greater is the release of prolactin. The less frequently suckling takes place, the less prolactin is produced, with the result that the growth of some of the egg-follicles in the ovary may occur and ovulation result. This explains the greater chance of ovulation occurring when women only breast feed par-tially, and when the baby is given semi-solid feeds and suckled less often.

Studies in many nations have shown that most non-lactating women resume ovulation and menstruation within three months of childbirth, but most lactating women delay ovulation and menstruation for between six and 10 months, or longer if they exclusively breast feed throughout. If they do not exclusively breast feed, giving solids in addition, ovulation may occur. For this reason women who breast feed would be wise to take contraceptive precautions. The choice of the method should be made by the woman in consultation with a doctor. If a hormonal contraceptive is chosen, the Pill should be avoided as there is some evidence that the oestrogen content reduces the supply of breast milk. This may not apply to the new low-dose oestrogen oral contraceptives. If a mother chooses to take the Pill, a small quantity of oestrogen and gestagen reaches the baby's body through the milk. It is without any effect on the baby's growth, development or behaviour.

A reduction in the quantity of milk does not occur if the gestagen-only pill (the Mini-pill) or an injectable gestagen, given at three-month intervals, is chosen. Studies have shown that gestagen may even increase the amount of milk produced. A small amount of gestagen is secreted in the milk. It has no deleterious effect on the baby's development or behaviour. As an alternative a woman may choose a non-hormonal method of contraception, such as a dia-phragm, or may decide to have an IUD placed in her uterus, methods which will not affect her milk supply.

DEMAND (NEED) FEEDING

What is meant by demand feeding?

Demand feeding implies that the baby is fed when he is hungry, when he needs or demands food. In 'scheduled' feeding the baby is fed at fixed times whether the baby is hungry or not. Babies are even woken up to be fed, and, of course, difficulties arise! It is like waking a man at 11 p.m. four hours after he has eaten a steak, and telling him he has to eat another steak! Some can, many cannot.

In most countries in the world, babies are fed on demand. The baby is carried about by his mother if she goes out, or sleeps near her if she is at home. When the baby indicates he wants to suckle or nuzzle her nipple, she offers it to him.

Demand feeding should start in hospital. For demand or need feeding to be successful the baby must 'room-in' with his mother. She is in close contact with him at all times, she cuddles him, plays with him, notes his changes in mood, and learns when his cry means hunger. From all these visual, tactile and emotional links, messages are carried to her brain, and the complex system which encourages milk secretion and its flow from her alveoli of the breasts to the collecting ducts is initiated. When the baby is hungry, the mother feeds him, changes him, pets him and then lets him sleep. A baby enjoys the breast. He nuzzles the nipples, his hands grasp the breast; and as he drinks his toes curl sensuously, his fingers move rhythmically, and in male babies erection of the penis is common. The mother notices these signs of contentment, she relaxes, and a further flow of milk occurs.

Demand, or need, feeding produces more milk and maintains lactation for longer than 'scheduled' feeding. With demand feeding the baby usually settles to his routine within three or four weeks.

DENTAL CARIES: BREAST FEEDING PROTECTS

I have heard that breast feeding protects the baby against dental caries: is this true?

Breast feeding is thought to protect a baby, in some way, against developing dental caries after his teeth have erupted. Why breast feeding is protective is not understood. It does not seem related to the baby's fluoride intake, which is greater in breast milk in areas where there are high levels of fluoride in drinking water. A possible reason is that the higher sugar content of formula milks may habituate the child to want sugar, in other words he develops a 'sweet tooth'. It is known that sugar is a factor in dental caries. Research workers have not been able to prove that sugar is the reason for the difference in the incidence of dental caries between breast-fed and bottle-fed babies. Another suggestion is that the higher selenium content of breast milk is a protective factor. As well, malocclusion (see below), which is more common in bottle-fed babies, may be a factor in dental caries.

We don't yet know why breast-fed babies have less dental caries than bottle-fed babies, but we do know that breast feeding helps to protect babies against dental decay.

DENTAL MALOCCLUSION

Will breast feeding my baby reduce its chance of having dental malocclusion?

Breast-fed babies suckle, and obtain the milk by squeezing the areola of the breast and the lower part of the nipple between tongue and hard palate, so that milk spurts out aided by the 'let-down' reflex. To effect this, the baby draws the mother's nipple deep into his mouth by moving his tongue backwards.

Bottle-fed babies push their tongues forward to control the amount of milk coming from the rubber teat and suck, so that they have a greater chance of swallowing air as well as milk.

There is evidence that breast-fed babies are less likely to have dental malocclusion (i.e. an abnormal relationship and contact between the upper and lower teeth) than bottle-fed babies. A study in Zimbabwe showed that only 0.3 per cent of black children who were breast fed for two or three years had an overshot maloccluded bite compared with 3 per cent of white children, who had usually been bottle fed.

A baby who breast feeds, pressing its jaws and face against its mother's breasts, receives more stimulation and uses more muscles than a bottle-fed baby. A bottle-fed baby does not suckle but sucks at the teat, using his tongue and fewer of his mouth muscles, which are relatively under-exercised. This under-use of the facial muscles may be a factor in dental malocclusion, but other factors, such as thumb sucking and the shape of the jaw bone may be involved.

DIETING AND BREAST FEEDING

If I go on a slimming diet, will my milk production diminish?

The answer to this question is that it depends on how strict the diet is, and how rigidly the mother keeps to it. Gimmicky, crash or quick weight-loss diets should be avoided as they act by producing malnourishment. If a sensible diet is chosen which limits fat intake and reduces the daily calorie intake, but makes sure that it is more than 1500kcal(6258kJ) and that the carbohydrate content is more than 100g, there should be no reduction in breast milk.

DROOPY BREASTS

If I breast feed will I develop 'droopy boobs'?

This question is really saying 'Will my breasts be erotically stimulating to myself and to others if I choose to breast feed?'

During pregnancy the breasts enlarge. This is due to the growth of the 'milk tree', particularly the ducts and the alveoli, and to fat laid down around the branches and tufts of the 'tree'. The increased weight of the breasts puts strain on the supporting bands of fibrous tissue which separate the breast lobes and are attached to the fibrous sheath which covers the pectoral muscle (see p. 18). If the supporting bands stretch, the breasts droop because of gravity. Pendulous or droopy breasts can be minimized by wearing a supporting bra during pregnancy and during lactation, but not prevented. Prevention depends on your heredity, on your weight (obese women tend to have bigger, droopy breasts) and on your age.

Droopy breasts are due more to these factors, and to the added influence of pregnancy, than to breast feeding. A woman who breast feeds reduces the amount of fat (including breast fat) she laid down in pregnancy more quickly than a woman who bottle feeds.

The answer to the question then is: breast feeding does *not* cause 'droopy boobs'. They are due to the influence of heredity, of body fat and to that of pregnancy, not to breast feeding.

DRUGS IN BREAST MILK

Are there any drugs which may be prescribed for me that I should avoid when breast feeding?

Drugs are often prescribed which have only a slight or a transient benefit, apart from a psychological one. When a woman is breast feeding, she should avoid this unnecessary medication.

Occasionally, a doctor may believe it necessary for a mother to take a particular drug even though it may be undesirable for her baby, as the drug is excreted in the breast milk. The problem of transfer to the baby can be minimized if the mother times the taking of the medication so that the baby is not fed when the level of the drug in the milk is at its peak. This usually occurs within one to one and a half hours after taking the drug by mouth.

Most drugs are excreted in milk, usually in small amounts, and neither harm nor benefit your baby. In the following list, drugs which may be harmful are noted. Some can be taken with caution when you are breast feeding. *Those marked with an asterisk should be avoided* (usually there is a substitute).

* Addictive narcotics	AVOID OR DON'T BREAST FEED. May cause addiction and severe withdrawals in baby.
Alcohol	Probably safe in small amounts, but not if you are a heavy drinker (more than six glasses (1000ml) a day of beer or equivalent; wine five glasses, whisky 180ml). If you drink too much you will be unable to care for – to mother – your baby properly. Also, your baby's brain is continuing to develop in the first two years of life, and it is possible that the alcohol may affect this development by damaging the nerve connections which are forming in the brain. (Small amounts of alcohol are harmless and may help if you are anxious about your skill as a parent.)

Anti-anxiety drugs (e.g. Valium and Serapax)	Some babies become lethargic if the mother is given Valium; but the drug is probably safe in small doses.
Antibiotics	Only small amounts of most antibiotics are transferred into the milk. Sensitization of the baby may occur, especially with the penicillins, but is very rare, and clinical need supersedes risk. The following antibiotics should be either avoided or taken with care:
*chloramphenicol (Chloromycetin)	Not used much. AVOID as it may destroy the baby's white blood cells.
kanamycin	If required by the mother, monitor baby for possible toxicity – rare.
nalidixic acid (Negram)	Used to treat urinary tract infections. If the mother has kidney failure the drug may reach a high concentration in the milk, otherwise safe.
nitrofurantoin (Furadantin)	Used to treat urinary tract infections. Avoid if you are from an eastern Mediterranean country, as you may have an enzyme deficiency which permits the drug to cause anaemia and jaundice.
streptomycin	May reach high concentrations in breast milk if mother's kidneys are failing. If this happens, may damage the baby's hearing. In most cases, safe.
sulfisoxazole (Gantrisan)	Avoid in first two weeks after childbirth as may cause kernicterus (jaundice of brainstem) in the baby.
*tetracyclines	Become incorporated into the baby's teeth causing damage to the dentine. AVOID.
*Anticoagulants	Except for heparin and warfarin, which are safe, AVOID all other anticoagulants as they may cause haemorrhages in the baby.

Anticonvulsants

One anticonvulsant, primidone (Mysoline), may reach high levels in the milk, and should not be taken as it causes lethargy in the baby. No reported problems with the others.

Antidepressants
(Tricyclics)

In the doses usually prescribed only a small amount of the drug is excreted in milk, and is probably harmless to the baby.

Antithyroid drugs

Until recently it was believed that propylthiouracil and carbimazole were secreted into breast milk at high concentrations in the mother's blood. Recent evidence suggests that it is not so. Until the matter is resolved, it is probably unwise for a mother taking these drugs to breast feed.

Aspirin

Used occasionally, it has no effect on baby. Used excessively it may cause skin rashes in the baby and, perhaps, small haemorrhages in its intestinal tract.

Barbiturates

Best avoided in most circumstances as they may stimulate the baby's liver enzymes and may cause drowsiness.

Bromides

Not prescribed much nowadays. In large doses may cause drowsiness and rashes in the baby.

Caffeine

Only insignificant amounts are excreted into breast milk. Caffeine has no effect on the baby if fewer than six cups of tea or coffee are taken each day. Heavy caffeine use by the mother may cause jitteriness in baby.

*Cancer therapy drugs (anti-metabolites)	These drugs kill cancer cells which are dividing frequently. Body cells which divide frequently, such as the blood cells and the cells lining the intestines, are also killed. AVOID BREAST FEEDING if taking these drugs.
Chloral hydrate	Best avoided as may cause drowsiness in the baby.
Cigarettes	More than 20 a day cause high levels of nicotine in the baby's fat. It is not known whether this is dangerous. It is best to avoid smoking if you can.
Cough mixtures containing potassium iodide	May affect baby's thyroid, causing cretinism if taken in large doses. In small doses probably safe but best avoided. If you are a cough mixture addict, do not breast feed.
Ergot preparations	Avoid unless absolutely needed as may cause vomiting or diarrhoea in the baby, or, rarely, a weak pulse and low blood pressure. A short course given in the first few weeks after childbirth to reduce uterine bleeding presents no problems.
Hypoglycaemic agents, oral (anti-diabetic drugs taken by mouth)	May cause low blood sugar in the baby, but this rarely occurs.
Laxatives	Stool softeners (e.g. Coloxyl, Metamucil and Isogel) have no effect on the baby when taken by the mother in normal doses. Laxatives (e.g. cascara, danthron, Doxidan) should be avoided as they are secreted into breast milk and may cause colic and diarrhoea. Senna (Sennokot) can be taken safely.
*Lead	Enters breast milk. Sometimes a component of skin ointments. AVOID.

Lithium
In large doses may make the baby cold, floppy and blue. Unlikely to be prescribed when a woman is lactating.

Metronidazole (Flagyl), tinidazole (Tinazol, Fasigyn)
Used to treat vaginal trichomoniasis. Secreted into breast milk, probably no effect on the baby. *Avoid taking the one-day large-dose regimen.*

Nicotine
Transmitted in breast milk. If the mother smokes more than 20 cigarettes a day may affect brain development. Try to avoid smoking.

Pesticides and herbicides
Certain pesticides and herbicides, particularly those containing dieldrin, DDT, hexachlorobenzine, pindone (and possibly 2,4,5,T), are absorbed into the human body when a person eats food which has been contaminated. Ninety per cent of pesticides get into the mother's body through food – the remaining 10 per cent from absorbing the chemical after spraying. Fatty foods, such as meat and dairy foods, contain the highest amounts; but pesticides can be absorbed from cereals, chicken, eggs, fruit and vegetables. In the human body the chemicals are taken up by fat cells and the greater the exposure to the pesticides, the greater the concentration of them in fat cells. The pesticides are transferred from the fatty tissue to milk. In a study in Queensland of Brisbane mothers, it was found that breast milk contained higher concentrations of all the pesticides mentioned earlier (except 2,4,5,T) than are regarded as 'safe' levels by US standards.

Most of the currently available information is about DDT, which is found in higher concentration in human milk than in cow's milk. No known damage to humans. It is probable that the DDT level reaches a 'steady state' while the baby is in the uterus, and the DDT in breast milk has no effect. Restrictions on the use of DDT in many countries has led to a fall in the concentration of DDT in breast milk.

Phenothiazines

All are secreted in breast milk, may cause drowsiness in the baby. (The proprietary names of the commonly used phenothiazines include: Largactil, Sparine, Stemetil, Trilafon.)

* Propanolol

Used to treat high blood pressure. It is secreted into breast milk and may cause heart failure in the baby. AVOID if possible or don't breast feed if it is essential for you to take the drug.

Radioactive substances (especially radioactive iodine)

AVOID as radioactive iodine may damage baby's thyroid gland

Reserpine

Occasionally used to treat high blood pressure. Causes stuffy nose in baby.

Steroids

The common steroids taken by lactating mothers are those contained in oral contraceptives. Most women avoid combined oral contraceptives but some women choose the gestagen-only Pill or injectables. The gestagen is secreted in breast milk in small amounts, but has no known effect on the baby.

Strontium-90

No problem in breast milk, but cow's milk may contain five times the amount of human milk.

DRUGS IN CHILDBIRTH AND SUCKLING

To what extent do pain-relieving drugs given during childbirth affect the baby's ability to suckle?

In Australia and Britain, pethidine is the most usual drug given to relieve pain in childbirth. Sometimes a sedative, such as diazepam (Valium) or promazine (Sparine), is also given. Each dose of pethidine varies from 50–200mg but usually a total of 100–200mg is given. In recent years the quantity of pethidine given has been reduced as epidural analgesia has become fashionable.

In the USA meperidine (pethidine) is often prescribed, together with promethazine (Phenergan), 50–100mg of the former being given every three to four hours during labour. Sparine (promazine) may be prescribed, as may barbiturates, although these are less used today than in the past. Valium (diazepam) is also prescribed in the USA to women in labour.

The effect of these drugs upon the newborn baby depends on the total dose given, the rapidity with which it is broken down in the body, the amount which crosses the placenta to enter the baby's circulation and the speed with which the baby 'detoxicates' and excretes the drug.

The babies of mothers who have been heavily sedated with barbiturates, or with diazepam, are likely to be slow to respond to stimuli, and slow to suckle. Today few mothers receive heavy sedation and the quantity of the drugs usually given during childbirth should have no significant effect on the baby.

The effect of pethidine is controversial. Some reports suggest that the baby of a mother who has been given pethidine in childbirth is drowsy and apathetic. Other reports show little alteration in the baby's ability to 'bond' and to suckle.

It does not appear to matter whether the pethidine is injected intravenously or into a muscle. The level of pethidine in the baby's cord blood measured at delivery is close to that in the mother's blood, indicating that pethidine is readily transferred. If mother and baby are healthy, it is probable that pethidine has no adverse affect on the baby, but if the pregnancy is complicated or the birth premature, pethidine may add to the baby's respiratory difficulties and to its ability to suckle.

Until the controversy regarding the effects on the baby of drugs given to the mother during childbirth is resolved, it is important for a mother to insist that she is told the type and quantity of the drugs she is given, and to have the right to choose not to have the drug. Good care in childbirth means finding a balance between pain relief for the mother and reducing the adverse effects of medications on the new baby.

If the baby is drowsy and apathetic as a result of medication given to the mother during childbirth, she should insist he is given to her to feed at frequent intervals. Even if the baby falls asleep while feeding, he can be fed again after a short interval.

DUMMIES (PACIFIERS)

Is it safe to give my baby a dummy (pacifier)?

Pacifiers or dummies have had a long history. At one time they were popular with mothers and recommended by doctors. Then doctors condemned them, pointing out that they were often dirty and unhygienic. They also observed, correctly, that a dummy coated with sugar given to an older child was a good way to rot his emerging teeth.

They are now back in fashion, but to be used with discretion. Most babies get comfort by sucking their thumbs. The thumb is probably cleaner and is certainly more natural than a dummy. But if your baby doesn't suck his thumb, it is better to let him suck a dummy than let him go on crying, provided you know he isn't hungry.

It is even better for you or his father to cuddle him. If that isn't possible offer him a dummy – with discretion.

ENGORGEMENT

How can a woman prevent her breasts becoming painful and swollen in the first days of lactation?

As your milk begins to be secreted into the alveoli following the prolactin stimulus, you will notice that your breasts suddenly become much larger. They won't stay that way, because once you have established breast feeding, they automatically adjust to a supply and demand situation. By then they will be producing two or three times as much milk as in the early days, but your baby will be hungrier and your 'let-down' reflex will be working more efficiently.

When your milk 'comes in' on the second or third day after birth, your breasts usually become swollen and rather tender. This is normal, but if the tenderness increases and the breasts become tensely swollen, they are said to be 'engorged'. Severe engorgement is painful and makes it difficult for your baby to feed. You can usually prevent severe engorgement by suckling your baby frequently for short periods of time before the milk 'comes in'.

When the milk 'comes in', and your breasts are mildly engorged, you can prevent the engorgement from becoming severe if you take the following actions:

● Express a little milk before putting your baby to the breast. The manoeuvre is described on page 45. The object is not really to express milk, but to stimulate the 'let-down' reflex which propels the milk along the ducts to the dilated parts under the areola. Once the milk begins to flow, the areola becomes less tense, and it is easier for your baby to get your nipple deep inside his mouth.

● Feed your baby at shorter intervals, for short periods of time, and make sure your breasts are empty by hand-expressing after each feed. If you prefer, you can use a breast pump.

● Because of the engorgement, the nipple may be insufficiently protractile to enable the baby to get it deep inside his mouth. The problem can be overcome by using a McCarthy (Mexican Hat) nipple shield or a thin latex nipple shield (Fig. 27). The part of the shield which covers the areola is made of soft plastic and the nipple extension is made of firmer plastic. When the baby sucks on the shield, a negative pressure is created which tends to draw the nipple into the nipple projection of the nipple shield. Studies have shown that the reduction in milk flow is less using the thin latex nipple shield than the Mexican Hat, but either is as effective in protecting the nipple from damage.

● If the engorgement is severe, more help is needed. Most midwives have their own particular method of treatment. Severe engorgement is due to a temporary excess of milk filling the alveoli but not being 'let-down' through the ducts. The dairy is overfull, but the milk trucks are on strike! The distension of the alveoli may also cause pressure and damage in the milk cells, with a resulting leakage of milk into the breast tissue surrounding the alveoli. As well, an intense congestion of blood occurs as the swollen alveoli press on and partially block the veins draining the lobules of the breasts. The result is that the breasts become painful, swollen, lumpy, tense and tender, with reddened skin.

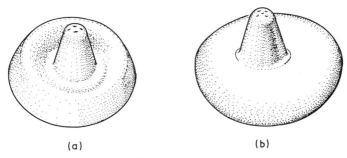

(a)   (b)

Fig. 27   Nursing nipple shields. (a) Mexican Hat; (b) Thin latex type (developed in the Department of Paediatrics, The John Radcliffe Hospital, Oxford)

If a mother can put up with the pain, and does nothing, the engorgement will subside after a few days, as the pressure in the alveoli prevents any further milk being made. In fact, this is one way of stopping lactation if a woman doesn't want to breast feed. But if you want to breast feed, you have to take action. The usual way that nurses deal with the problem is to place ice packs on the engorged breasts, or to apply hot and cold compresses (made by soaking a face flannel in hot or cold water and then wringing it out). This stimulates the blood to drain from the congested blood vessels and triggers the 'let-down' reflex.

Some midwives also suggest taking a shower and, while under it, trying to express some milk by hand-expression. The advantage of a shower is that the hot and cold water stimulate the blood flow, and the water jets stimulate the 'let-down' reflex. Hand-expression is not difficult to learn and will soften the breast sufficiently for the baby to take your nipple deeply inside his mouth.

Another way to start the milk flowing is to use a breast pump. Most hospitals have an electric breast pump (the usual one is called the Egnell Pump) and this is fairly efficient. It works by applying gentle suction and intermittent pressure on the areola, mimicking the baby's chewing motions. Cheaper breast pumps which operate solely by suction should be used carefully or you will get painful nipples. A novel kind of breast pump has been devised in Australia. The pump (called the Ellis Expressor) is water powered and connects with a household tap. It is cheap and has few maintenance problems. It can be used to express milk for preterm babies, who are not sufficiently strong to breast feed, or for relieving a blocked duct, as well as for treating severe engorgement.

The effectiveness of the breast pump is increased if the woman uses an oxytocin nasal spray (once in each nostril) before the procedure. The oxytocin encourages the 'let-down' reflex. Oxytocin nasal sprays are obtainable on prescription.

Another method of treating engorged breasts is to use a vibrator. The advantage of the vibrator is that whereas hand-massage hurts, the vibrator can be used in gentle stroking movements, from chest towards nipple, barely touching the skin but providing relief. It is so gentle there is no pain.

It is well to remember that most women will not get severely engorged breasts if they insist on feeding often, including at night, before and during the time the milk is 'coming-in'.

Engorgement is not due to excessive milk production caused by a raised prolactin level, it is due to a poorly stimulated 'let-down' reflex. The 'let-down' reflex becomes more efficient the more frequently a woman stimulates it by suckling her baby.

In cases of severe engorgement, many doctors recommend that the mother stops suckling the baby and hand-expresses the milk. Many mothers disagree, saying that it hurts more to express the breast than having the baby feed from it. As well, some paediatricians may prescribe bromocriptine, which inhibits prolactin release and so cuts down milk secretion. Provided a mother continues to stimulate her breasts by expressing, the temporary inhibition of prolactin release will not lead to failure of lactation.

Finally, if a mother develops a fever when her breasts are engorged, it may mean that she has mastitis: treatment is needed urgently (see p. 74).

EPISODIC CRYING

I wonder is my baby the only baby that seems to have prolonged spells of crying. My friends seem to have placid, docile babies – but mine cries episodically. I get distressed, anxious, resentful and often angry. Is it my fault? Am I a failure as a mother, or is the baby ill?

In a survey carried out in New South Wales, of the way women adjust to parenthood, one of the main anxieties expressed by mothers was that their babies had frequent periods of crying. One mother wrote: 'We weren't prepared for a baby who cried constantly day in, day out. Nothing seemed to make her happy.' Another mother said: 'It is as if you try everything and his face still puckers up and he sobs and seems to reject you. . . .' Another wrote: 'I find the crying remains in my head, I can even hear it when she is quiet.' The mothers observed that although most crying babies cried in episodic bursts in the late afternoons or evenings, episodic crying could occur at any time of the day or night. Because doctors don't know the cause of episodic crying and like to give a complaint a label, frequently the crying has been diagnosed as due to 'colic' or 'wind'. When episodic crying persists for days or weeks, the mother becomes anxious that she is an inadequate mother or resentful that the baby won't respond to her care. In some instances she argues that the baby must have some obscure illness which the doctor has failed to diagnose. As well she becomes increasingly fatigued, and believes that she is to blame for her baby's crying behaviour. She is not to blame. Babies cry because it is the only way that they can communicate. They cry from hunger, they cry from pain, they cry because they are bored, they cry because they are cold or wet, they cry because they have been overstimulated. It is often difficult for a mother to decide which of the many reasons is the cause for her baby's episodic crying.

Episodic crying is not likely to be due to colic or wind, nor is it usually associated with allergy or any disease. As the cause is not known, it follows that many 'treatments' are offered, some by doctors and many by folk-medicine. An advantage of trying the remedies is that the mother feels that she is doing something to help her baby. This helps her to relax. It is possible that if she is tense her baby notices it and becomes more tense himself and continues to cry.

There are various ways of trying to bring relief to a crying baby.

He may settle if he is given a feed or a dummy. He may settle if he is given a bath or, if he usually objects to bathing, he may prefer to be wrapped in a cuddly rug. Many mothers have found that motion helps, particularly if the motion causes vibrations. 'The only way we could get Simon to settle was to go for a drive in the car. Almost instantly he fell asleep and we had peace,' a mother wrote.

Recently mothers have tried massaging the baby gently, while talking to him. Those mothers who have used baby massage say that the baby becomes relaxed and calm, and that they prefer this technique to the methods outlined earlier.

If your baby has episodic crying you should check:

● Is he hungry? If he is, feed him.

● Is he wet or uncomfortable? If he is, change him.

● Is he bored? If he is, stimulate him.

● Is he noticing that you are tense, hurried and anxious? If so, do some deep breathing to calm down, cuddle him, and do what you have to do at a slower pace.

● Has he got 'wind'? If you believe he has, sit him up on your knee, talk to him and see if he burps.

Parents should expect that from time to time they will feel resentful, angry and hostile to their crying baby. 'How many times I wanted to throw Samantha in the creek and jump in after her. . . . Then she'd be quiet for a time and I'd look at her angelic face and wonder how I ever thought of such a thing,' one mother wrote. Another said: 'We both loved our baby but there were times when we could cheerfully have locked her away out of earshot during her crying episodes.' It is normal (and helpful, even if it sounds cruel) in times of stress to put the baby in a separate room for a short time, shut the door, turn up the radio or record player, and begin to relax.

Perhaps the greatest help is to have a husband, a relative or a friend who will look after the baby periodically so that the mother gets a break. This is the doula concept, or 'mothering the mother'. A mother who is under stress, who is anxious that she isn't coping with her baby and who is fatigued needs support from those around her so that she can regain her confidence in her mothering.

Episodic crying tends to be self-limiting and the evening variety nearly always ceases after three months – which is why it has been labelled 'three-month colic'. The all-day variety tends to persist for longer.

FAILURE TO THRIVE

My baby is a slow feeder and always very sleepy. He wants to be fed only every four or five hours and sleeps for 12 hours at night. In the past four weeks he hasn't gained any weight. I offered him complementary feeds but he wasn't interested.

Failure of a healthy breast-fed baby to thrive is unusual, but it happens from time to time. The cause is unknown. With a sleepy, contented baby, the mother may interpret 'demand feeding' too strictly, and underfeed her baby. This is what has happened to the baby in this question. Some babies who fail to thrive have hidden infections or are ill, so it would be wise to have the baby checked by a doctor. Illness is not likely in the baby in the question as he is so contented. As the baby only feeds four times a day he has become undernourished, and possibly dehydrated.

One way of coping with this problem is to wake him more often (gently jack-knifing him several times, by bending his head towards his feet as you hold him in your arms, seems to work) and offer him a feed. If this does not resolve the problem or if he becomes lethargic and dehydrated he may need to be admitted to hospital for re-hydration.

FEEDS: COMPLEMENTARY AND SUPPLEMENTARY

What is the difference between a complementary and a supplementary feed?

A complementary feed is one in which formula milk (or donated breast milk) is given to complement the insufficient amount of the breast feed. It should be given from a spoon rather than a bottle. A supplementary feed is a formula feed given in place of a breast feed.

FIGHTING AT THE BREAST

My baby seems to fight with me when I try to feed him. Why?

From time to time some babies appear to fight at the breast. This may be due to frustration because the breast is too full and the baby can't get the nipple comfortably in his mouth. The solution is to hand-express a little milk before you feed the baby.

Some mothers who have 'fighting babies' find it helpful to express some breast milk and to give it through a teat first. When the baby takes the teat into his mouth, let him drink and then substitute your nipple for the teat nipple. But this method means that you have the trouble of cleaning and sterilizing bottles and teats.

In other cases, fighting may be due to the memory of being unable to breathe when he was feeding. If a mother does not support her breast properly, so that it falls over the baby's nose, suffocating him, he may become frightened. He may remember the feeling of suffocation, and fight. It is important to remember to give him 'air-space', so that he can breathe easily when he feeds, by pressing your breast with your finger to keep it clear of his nose (Fig. 28).

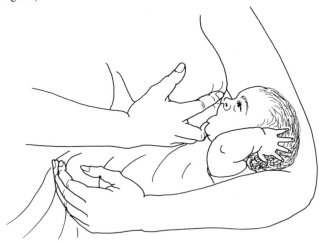

Fig. 28   Allowing the baby 'air-space' while feeding. Note how the mother holds her baby allowing the breast tissue to be pressed away

Some babies play rather than fight, but they play very vigorously, like young calves, butting and grabbing the nipple, until the milk flows freely, when they feed contentedly.

It is probably best to avoid giving the baby a sedative (such as chloral hydrate), which is advised by some doctors.

FLUORIDE

Should I give my baby fluoride when I breast feed to prevent later dental caries?

In many places the drinking water has had fluoride added (fluoridation). A pregnant or lactating woman will obtain all the fluoride she needs from the water she drinks. When she breast feeds her baby, fluoride is transferred through the milk. The quantity is low but sufficient to protect the baby's unerupted teeth, as far as can be judged at present. Fluoride supplements are not needed in the first six months of life.

The problem is very complex, as dental caries are caused by many factors. A lack of fluoride is one, and another is claimed to be the intake of sugar-rich foods from an early age. Dental caries may be encouraged by the habit of some mothers of filling a feeding bottle with sweetened fruit juice or vitamin syrups, and giving it at night as a 'comforter'. The child, usually under three years of age, sleeps with the teat in its mouth, and a slow seepage of sugar-rich fluid occurs.

On the positive side, several studies in Britain and the USA have shown a lower incidence of dental caries in the teeth of breast-fed as compared to bottle-fed babies. This may be due more to the preventive dental measures taken by breast-feeding mothers once breast feeding is discontinued, rather than to the type of feeding in the first months of the baby's life.

FORMULA FEEDING

I propose to stop breast feeding and start bottle feeding: should I choose any particular milk?

Bottle feeding uses what is called a formula milk. All formula milks are based on cow's milk which has been adapted or modified by the manufacturer to resemble human milk, both in the quantity and in the proportions of its nutritional content. Surprisingly, an investigation in a rural area of Britain in 1977, showed that 68 per cent of the mothers were unaware that formula or artificial milks were prepared from cow's milk.

Formula milks were introduced into infant feeding about 60 years ago. They largely replaced raw cow's milk, which was made suitable for small babies by diluting it and adding sugar. The manufacturers of formula milks devised several forms of modified cow's milk. It could be obtained as liquid condensed milk, evaporated milk or as dry powdered milk. These preparations, manufactured under strict hygienic control, were much safer for the baby than raw cow's milk, provided that the mother used reasonable cleanliness to prepare the formula and followed the manufacturers' directions precisely.

The market for formula milk expanded rapidly and soon a large number of formula milks became available. Currently, over 50 different formula milks are available, each differing slightly in composition. Because of the wide range available, a mother may wish to be guided by a doctor or a nurse on her choice of formula milk.

A further factor is the cost of the formula milk: this may induce a mother to select the cheapest formula feed which is usually the least 'humanized'. Such milks may lack adequate amounts of essential fatty acids and may be positively disadvantageous to the growth and mental development of young babies. These milks are not only not as good as, but are less safe than human milk.

Although some women choose the cheapest formula milk, most choose the formula on the advice of other mothers or because of advertising.

In many developing countries sweetened condensed milk is used widely as a baby food by less educated, poorer mothers. The use is encouraged by advertisements and by labelling on the tins of the milk as 'recommended for feeding'. Sweetened condensed milk is not suitable for baby feeding. If it is diluted 1 in 8 it contains rather more protein, half as much fat and considerably more sugar than human milk; while if it is diluted 1 in 5 (as most manufacturers recommend) it contains twice as much protein, twice as much sugar and less fat than human milk. As well, sweetened condensed milks have high mineral levels which could place a strain on the baby's kidneys, as could the extra protein. The 1 in 5 dilution provides an amount of energy comparable with that of human milk but too little fat and too much protein, while the 1 in 8 dilution provides too little energy and fat.

In addition, sweetened condensed milk is deficient in vitamin A, and this can lead to keratomalacia of the infant's eyes and blindness. It is believed that sweetened condensed milk has been responsible for thousands of cases of preventable blindness in Asia.

In contrast, the formula milks available to women in the developed nations are manufactured under hygienic conditions and are modified appropriately to resemble human milk. If a woman is unable to breast feed or chooses not to breast feed, she can choose a satisfactory substitute from the range of formula milks available.

FORMULA MILK: PREPARATION

How important is the proper preparation of formula milk?

Cleanliness is important in preparing the bottle feed, as bottle-fed babies resist infections less efficiently than breast-fed babies. The formula milk itself is unlikely to contain any bacteria when purchased, but bacteria can be introduced by failing to keep the lid firmly closed on the tin or carton. The person preparing the feed must make sure that no contamination occurs. The spoon and the measuring jug (if one is used for measuring the water or mixing the feed) should have been boiled or scalded before use, and should be washed carefully after use. The water needed for diluting evaporated milk or for mixing with the powdered milk should have been boiled.

The feeding bottle and teats must be sterilized before the feed is prepared. The bottle and teats are rinsed in cold running water, then cleaned inside several times, again in cold running water. They are then immersed in a diluted sterilizing solution which contains chlorine (for example Milton or Simpla Tablets) and left until the next feed is prepared. When this is ready, the bottle and teats are removed from the sterilizing solution and washed with running water. The alternative is to clean the bottle and teats after feeding and to boil them in a saucepan for 10 minutes. After each feed, the bottle and the teats are cleaned and the process repeated. In the USA and some other countries, disposable, pre-sterilized plastic bottles are available which can replace the traditional glass resterilizable bottles.

FORMULA PREPARATION MISTAKES

How can I be sure that I am preparing the formula feed properly?

Baby-food manufacturers give instructions on their cartons and tins on how to prepare the formula correctly. If the directions are followed exactly, the resulting formula will be correctly made. Unfortunately, a number of mothers do not prepare the formula feeds correctly. In a study in Britain in 1977 by the Department of Health and Social Security, it was found that 11 per cent of mothers were making the mixture too concentrated, so the babies were getting extra calories, a cause of infantile obesity. Another survey in London, two years earlier, showed that only 46 per cent of mothers were measuring the milk powder correctly, using the milk scoop provided, and only 43 per cent added the recommended amount of sugar. When both the amounts of milk powder and sugar used were considered, only 23 per cent of women followed the manufacturer's instructions exactly. Many of the errors made by the mothers were minor, but 21 per cent – one mother in five – made a serious error in preparing the powdered or evaporated milk chosen by her. In addition, nine per cent of the mothers used fresh cow's milk, usually incorrectly diluted, and containing too high a concentration of salt for a small baby.

GOING OUT

Breast feeding can become a 'bind' if the mother wants to go out for the evening and leave her baby at home. Is there any alternative to asking the baby-sitter to give the baby a bottle of formula milk?

There is no reason why breast feeding should markedly restrict a woman's social life, provided she doesn't want to go out too often. In many cases she can take her baby with her and feed it when it needs feeding. In some situations this is clearly impossible, but she can ensure that the baby is exclusively fed on breast milk in one of two ways. First, she can hand-express her milk after each feed, and second, if she is one of the 20 per cent of women who produce drip milk, she can collect the milk which drips from the other breast during feeds. This method is more convenient and is easier if she purchases a 'drip-milk' collector (Eschman, England).

The collector is shaped like a nipple shield and is a hollow plastic container, the lid of which can be unscrewed. Alternatively, a plastic container with a tight lid, or a plastic baby bottle may be used. Prior to use the container, the collector and the plastic bottle are sterilized in Milton, and then washed. The drip milk collects during the feed and is poured from the collector into the bottle at the end of the feed. About 80 to 100ml of milk will drip over a 24-hour period. Breast milk, whether obtained by hand expression or by drip, can be kept safely in a domestic refrigerator for 24 hours, but if it is intended to obtain a stock of breast milk, it should be frozen and kept in the freezer, when it can be used safely for up to 21 days.

Chilled milk normally separates into two layers, and the milk should be reconstituted by inverting the container several times before offering it to the baby. To freeze milk, it is first chilled in the refrigerator and then placed in the coldest part of the freezer. When you want to use it, you should thaw the milk quickly by placing it under running cold water. Once the milk has liquefied, it is warmed to body temperature and given to the baby. If you give your expressed milk to your baby it is not necessary to boil the milk.

When the mother wants to go out, missing an expected feed, the expressed milk is available for her baby and is given by spoon or feeding bottle.

HAND EXPRESSION

How can I learn to hand-express my milk?

The technique is relatively simple but until you have become adept you may find that only a tiny drop of milk appears on your nipple (Fig. 29). You must be gentle when you hand-express. If it hurts, you are not doing it properly.

- Cup your breast in your hand. Usually you will find it easier if you use your right hand for your left breast and vice versa.

- Put your thumb above the nipple at the edge of the areola and your forefinger underneath the nipple at the edge of the areola.

- If you feel gently around the edge of the areola and towards the nipple you will notice small lumpy areas, where milk has collected in the milk-duct reservoirs.

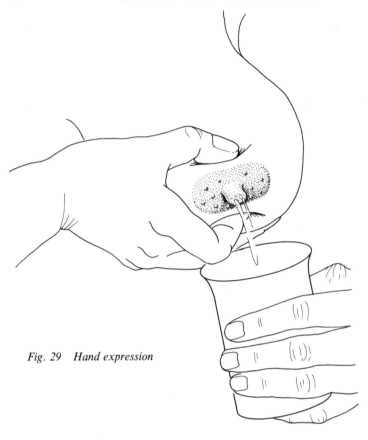

Fig. 29   Hand expression

- Press inwards and backwards towards your chest with your finger and thumb and squeeze the reservoirs gently, intermittently, rotating your hand so that all the reservoirs are squeezed. Don't slide your fingers towards the nipple as this doesn't help.

- The intermittent squeezing action should lead to milk squirting from your nipples, to be collected in a clean container, as your 'let-down' reflex begins to work.

- When the engorgement is less, and the area round your areola is soft, offer your breast to your baby.

IRON SUPPLEMENTS

Do breast-fed babies need iron supplements in the first six months of life?

If the mother has eaten a balanced diet during pregnancy, containing meat and dark-green leafy vegetables, by the end of pregnancy her baby will have received about 300mg of iron, mainly in the last 10 weeks. (Obviously a preterm (premature) baby receives less iron.) Most of the iron is stored in the baby's liver and is available to meet its need for iron in the first months of its life. In addition, if the umbilical cord is not clamped for two minutes after birth, the baby gets a small transfusion which adds another 60ml of blood, containing about 15mg of iron to its stores.

A baby needs iron to add to the haemoglobin in its increasing blood volume, and for its increasing muscle mass. As well, a baby loses some iron (as we all do) in the cells which are constantly shed from the intestines, the skin, the hair and the nails.

It is difficult to calculate the exact amount of iron required by a baby, which is why there is controversy among experts. The amount required may be as little as 0.5–1.0mg a day or as much as 6mg a day. Breast milk contains an average of 0.5mg to 1.5mg of iron per litre, a quantity a baby doesn't drink until he is between three and six months old. Only half of this iron is absorbed from the intestines into the baby's blood.

Those paediatricians who believe that a baby needs less than 1.0mg of iron each day say that a breast-fed baby gets enough iron in the milk it drinks and by using up some of its stored iron. They point out that most babies fully breast fed for five to six months are not anaemic and that solids added after five to six months contain iron, so that anaemia is probably prevented. They also point out that iron should not be given in the first nine weeks of life as it is poorly absorbed, and after that time may 'saturate' the transporting protein, lactoferrin, interfering with its anti-infective properties. A study in Finland supports this opinion. The iron status of 238 healthy newborn babies was studied from birth to 12 months of age. No evidence of anaemia was found among the babies, and their iron stores remained reasonably full. It was concluded that up to six months of age supplemental iron was not needed, but that iron should be considered for breast-fed infants after six months of age, and should be given to babies exclusively breast fed for more than nine months.

Iron is obtained from meat, liver and vegetables, and if the baby is given these foods in addition to breast milk from about six months of age, the need for supplemental iron is less.

Other paediatricians reject this view, noting that anaemia affects about 20 per cent of babies aged one to two in the USA (mainly in poor families). The Committee on Nutrition of the American Academy of Pediatrics has calculated that a baby may require as much as 270mg of additional iron during his first year of life. This represents an average of 0.7mg of iron a day. Although most babies obtain a fair amount of iron from milk (and later from solids), the Committee recommends that all full-term babies are given an intake of iron of 1mg per kilogram of body-weight each day from three months of age, and preterm babies are given twice that amount from the second month of life. It is claimed that this amount of iron will not saturate all the lactoferrin, and that anaemia will be prevented.

The matter is controversial but if you believe that your baby should be given iron, or your doctor recommends that he should be given iron, iron preparations are available. Two often used (which also contain vitamin C) are Ferrous Fumarate Mixture BPC (also called Fersamal Syrup) and Ferrous Sulphate Mixture BPC. The dose is 5ml of the former and 2ml of the latter each day. This provides between 12 and 25mg of elemental iron, of which the baby will absorb about one-quarter.

It is questionable if this amount is needed. My calculations suggest that if iron is needed at all by breast-fed babies, 3.5mg of elemental iron each day is enough, beginning at the third or fourth month of life.

These comments refer to term babies of healthy mothers. If a mother has been anaemic in pregnancy or her baby is preterm (that is, born before the 37th week) iron supplements will be required, as its body stores of iron will not have been built up.

JAUNDICE AND BREAST FEEDING

I have read that a complication of breast feeding is that some babies become jaundiced. Is this true?

In the body there is a constant breakdown and renewal of red blood cells. A result of red-cell breakdown is the accumulation in the blood of a substance called bilirubin. Bilirubin is acted on by an enzyme (glucuronyl transferase) and excreted in the urine. If too much bilirubin is formed, or if there is insufficient enzyme to act on it, jaundice may result.

In the first days of life, most babies have some degree of 'physiological' jaundice caused by an increased load of bilirubin on the liver's enzyme system. This is due to the breakdown of fetal red blood cells which are no longer needed now that the baby has been born. Physiological jaundice usually diminishes and disappears by the fifth to seventh day of life. Breast-fed babies are no more likely to develop physiological jaundice than are formula-fed babies.

In a few breast-fed babies, a substance called pregnanediol is excreted in the mother's milk. It is not known why this happens. Pregnanediol competes in the baby's liver for the enzyme which acts on bilirubin, with the result that insufficient enzyme is available to deal with the bilirubin. This means that the baby may become jaundiced when it is about seven days old. The jaundice may persist in a mild form for a number of weeks.

About one baby in every 250 is affected by 'breast-milk jaundice', and a mother whose first baby is affected has a 70 per cent chance of breast-milk jaundice in a subsequent baby.

Breast feeding can continue in spite of the jaundice, but the doctor will need to check the level of bilirubin in the baby's blood at intervals. If it rises above 260mmol/litre the mother should stop breast feeding for about 48 hours. Breast-feeding jaundice is not associated with brain damage (kernicterus) and causes no harm to the baby.

LACTATION AND BREAST FEEDING

Is lactation the same as breast feeding?
Lactation is the physiological process which leads to the secretion of milk in the alveoli of the female breast, its passage along the milk ducts due to the 'let-down' reflex and its ejection into the mouth of the baby by sucking.

Breast feeding comprises more than lactation: it adds the interaction between mother and baby; her response to his signals and his response to hers; the tactile contact between the couple; and the ingestion of the milk by the baby.

Breast feeding helps women to make closer contact with their own

bodies (if they haven't learnt to do this earlier) and to recognize that
their bodies are 'good'.

LACTATION SUPPRESSION

How can I stop lactating?

The most natural way to stop lactating is by weaning, that is by
giving your baby fewer and fewer breast feeds. The lack of the
stimulus of breast feeding reduces the prolactin reflex and the milk
slowly ceases to be produced.

A large number of women either choose not to breast feed or,
having started, give up suddenly for various reasons. In these cases
the natural method of weaning is inapplicable.

Two methods are available to inhibit or suppress lactation.

The first is just to stop breast feeding. Quite quickly the breasts
become engorged with milk and the pressure of the secreted milk in
the alveoli prevents more milk being secreted. In addition, without
the baby sucking, the prolactin reflex ceases, so that the milk cells
cease to produce milk. As the breasts become swollen, tender and
painful, a good supporting bra is needed, and most mothers require
analgesics because of the pain. Contrary to folklore, there is no need
to restrict the fluid intake, to bind the breasts, or to take laxatives.

The second method relies on the fact that continued milk secretion
depends on the prolactin reflex. A drug which prevents the secretion
of prolactin should prevent lactation starting, and 'dry up' lactating
breasts. Such a drug is now available: it is called bromocriptine and
needs to be taken for about 14 days to 'dry up' the breasts.

Until bromocriptine became available, oestrogens (synthetic
female sex hormones) were used to stop lactation. In appropriate
doses, taken for seven to 10 days, oestrogens were quite successful,
but in one-third of women the breasts filled up again a week or so
after completing treatment. About 10 years ago, doctors became
concerned that oestrogens used to suppress lactation, particularly if
taken in the two or three weeks immediately after childbirth, increased the chance that a mother might develop a clot in a vein, or
even a pulmonary embolus. These events were more likely to occur
if the woman was overweight, over thirty, smoked and had been
delivered by forceps or caesarean section. The problem did not seem
to occur when women decided to suppress lactation at a later time.

Another concern of some women is that oestrogens (particularly DES) taken to suppress lactation might induce cancer. This concern has arisen because of the known relationship between DES *taken in large doses* by mothers threatening to abort and vaginal cancer in some of their daughters about 18 years later. Oestrogens, including DES, in the doses used for suppressing lactation will not provoke cancer, and can be used relatively safely to suppress lactation, but today, bromocriptine is preferred.

'LET-DOWN' REFLEX PAINFUL

Sometimes my 'let-down' reflex, which is particularly strong, occurs and I get a severe pain in my breast as the milk is ejected.

The reason for excessive 'let-down', which has been described as the feeling that the 'tiny ducts are bursting with the pressure of a tidal wave of milk coming down' is obscure.

If it occurs, try to relax: the more tense you are the more you will feel it.

MEDICAL DISEASES AND BREAST FEEDING

Does any medical disease make it unwise for a mother to breast feed?

Very few chronic illnesses are contra-indications to breast feeding. If a mother has advanced (terminal) cancer or severe kidney disease she may feel too ill to breast feed, but it is rare for women with these illnesses to become pregnant or 'carry' the baby to term.

A woman who has active pulmonary tuberculosis should not breast feed until the injection of BCG given to her newborn baby has protected him, and the baby should be given an anti-tuberculosis drug such as isoniazid (INH) for the first year of his life.

If a breast-feeding mother has an acute illness such as a virus pneumonia, she may feel too ill to breast feed for a few days. During the illness the quantity of breast milk will diminish, and if she is not breast feeding the milk should be hand-expressed (or expressed using a breast pump) to prevent engorgement and to maintain lactation.

If a mother develops an infectious disease, such as mumps or measles, she can continue feeding as the diseases are most infectious before there are any clinical signs.

A mother who has frequent epileptic attacks, or who has a significant psychological problem, may find it wise not to breast feed, but
the decision should only be made after discussion with a doctor.

MENSTRUATION AND BREAST FEEDING

Why do my periods usually not return when I am breast feeding?

Lactation is initiated and maintained by prolactin, which is
released in response to suckling and by the 'let-down' reflex which
propels the milk to the nipple. During lactation the blood levels of
prolactin are higher than in women who are not lactating. Raised
levels of prolactin interfere with the release of the hormones (the
gonadotrophins) which control ovulation and menstruation, and
prevent the ovaries from responding to them. The effect of this is
that a breast-feeding mother's menstrual periods are usually sup-
pressed for about 20 weeks after childbirth. However, the level of
prolactin in the blood fluctuates during the day and in some women
may fall sufficiently to permit the release of some quantities of
gonadotrophin, with the result that menstruation starts again.
Usually the woman is not exclusively breast feeding and has reduced
the number of times she suckles her baby.

Menstruation is not a reason for stopping breast feeding – it has
no effect on the quality, nor the quantity of the breast milk.

A second question that is sometimes asked is: Can a woman
continue to breast feed if she becomes pregnant? Again, the answer
is that she can if she wishes. It will not damage her fetus in any way,
or deprive it of nourishment.

MILK ALLERGIES

*What are milk allergies? What is the likelihood of my baby developing
one of them?*

Milk allergies include infantile eczema (also called atopic dermatitis), asthma, and gastro-intestinal allergy, which shows as vomiting, diarrhoea and colic.

Several factors are involved in the development of milk allergy in
babies and young children. The most common cause is an inherited
defect, which affects about three babies in every 100. The defect

leads to the production by the baby of excessive amounts of a substance called immunoglobulin E, which sensitizes the cells which
make up the skin (and, probably, the lining cells of the intestines) to
the action of 'foreign protein'. If a baby who has been sensitized is
then exposed, in the first five or six months of life, to foreign protein
antigens, in the form of cow's milk protein, egg-white protein, protein in house dust or house-mite protein, the foreign protein may
react with the sensitized cells, with the result that eczema, asthma or
gastro-intestinal allergy results.

Most babies are protected against becoming allergic by two mechanisms. First, because they only form small amounts of immunoglobulin E their 'surface cells' (skin, intestines or lungs) are
not sensitized so much, or at all. The second mechanism is that the
babies are able to form a protective 'coating' over the surface of the
cells which line their intestines and lungs. This coat prevents them
absorbing the foreign protein which produces the allergy. The protective coat is a substance called secretory immunoglobulin A, or
sIgA for short. Secretory IgA coats the intestinal cells in normal
babies, but babies who have an inherited defect (in other words,
those where one of the parents is allergic) have a poor capacity to
make secretory IgA, so the foreign protein may be absorbed. Cow's
milk protein and egg-white protein are absorbed through the intestinal cells, while house-dust protein and house-mite protein are
absorbed through the cells lining the lungs. Once absorbed, the protein reacts with those cells in the child's body which have been sensitized by immunoglobulin E. The result is infantile eczema and, later,
asthma or gastro-intestinal colic.

Non-allergic babies make the protective secretory IgA within the
first six weeks of life, but allergic babies take longer, needing between
four and six months to produce sufficient secretory IgA to coat the
cells.

Infantile eczema is the most common allergy, and children whose
parents are allergic (that is, have hay fever or asthma) are more
likely to develop a milk allergy (especially eczema) than children of
non-allergic parents. Over half of babies who have one allergic parent
are likely to develop eczema unless precautions are taken.

Cow's milk protein is the cause of the allergy in about one-third
of children who develop infantile eczema, and in over half of the
children who develop gastro-intestinal allergies. This finding is supported by the evidence that these allergies are unusual in countries

where most babies are exclusively breast fed.

If a baby is exclusively breast fed from birth, the mother's milk provides the secretory IgA which protects him until he begins to make his own. But a baby who is fed on formula cow's milk, or is given occasional cow's milk feeds, or is given solids based on cow's milk early in life, may develop a milk allergy. The allergy may also occur in sensitized babies if the baby is given complementary feeds of formula cow's milk to prevent him crying at night when still in the maternity hospital.

Doctors have found that infantile eczema is reduced from over 40 per cent to under 6 per cent in allergic families, if the baby is exclusively fed on breast milk for the first six months of life and if contact with house mites and dust is reduced as far as possible. The incidence of childhood asthma is also reduced in babies who are exclusively breast fed for at least the first four months of life. In the opinion of one expert, Dr Goldman: 'The prevention of these sensitivities in children could be accomplished by encouraging breast feeding and thereby avoiding exposure to cow's milk. It is, therefore, evident that breast feeding and the avoidance of cow's milk is the most practical way of preventing the occurrence of cow's milk allergy in children.'

Interestingly, it has recently been reported from Scandinavia that a few exclusively breast-fed babies develop an allergic 'colic'. When the problem was investigated it was found that the mother had eaten a cow's milk product, such as cheese, or was drinking cow's milk. When she eliminated the particular product from her diet, the baby ceased to have colic. In a very few cases, other foods have produced the same effect.

Compared with bottle-fed babies, allergies in breast-fed babies are uncommon, unless the baby has been given complementary feeds of formula cow's milk or solids. Over half of allergic bottle-fed babies develop allergic diseases (particularly eczema and asthma) by the age of six, compared with less than one child in seven who is exclusively breast fed, or given soy-bean milk, in the first six months of life.

Milk allergies can largely be avoided if all babies are exclusively breast fed for the first five to six months of life (preferably the latter); and if solids are not started before this time. This means that nurses in maternity wards should not give newborn babies feeds of formula milk to prevent them crying at night when they are in the nursery without first discussing the matter with the mother and her doctor. In allergic families this advice is especially important, and if the mother is unwilling or unable to breast feed or if her milk is insufficient, a formula milk based on soy bean should be chosen. Soybean powder formulas include: Sobee, Prosobee and Velactin. Of these formula milks, Sobee and Prosobee require no supplementation with vitamins or with minerals, but Velactin requires additional vitamins and minerals. The quantities of each needed is clearly stated on the package.

As an alternative infant food for allergic babies, goat's milk may be chosen. The milk should be pasteurized or boiled before giving it to the baby, because of possible contamination with bacteria. So that the goat's milk resembles human milk in the proportion of its constituents, it should be diluted to three-quarters strength and 3.5g of sugar per litre added. The baby will require vitamin supplements in addition, as water-soluble vitamins in the milk are destroyed by pasteurization or boiling.

MILK: CALCIUM CONTENT

Cow's milk is said to contain three times the calcium content of human milk. Calcium makes strong bones, so it would surely be better if I gave my baby 'bottle' formula milk.

Paradoxically, it wouldn't. This is because the calcium in cow's milk combines with one of the fatty acids in the milk to form a soapy substance which is poorly absorbed from the baby's gut. As well, cow's milk contains less lactose than human milk, a lack which reduces the absorption of calcium. It is known that a number of babies fed from birth on cow's milk develop convulsions or tetany in the first two weeks of life. In about one-third of them the cause is lack of calcium in the blood (hypocalcaemia). Hypocalcaemia occurs very rarely in breast-fed babies.

MILK: CONSUMPTION

How much milk does an average baby need each day?

There is no 'average' baby, and babies' needs differ widely. The following table gives a mother some idea of a baby's needs for milk.

:age amount is given, and the range which covers the needs
babies is shown in brackets. These values are given in milli-
il) of milk per kilogram (kg) of the baby's body-weight
each day.

Age	Average amount of milk (ml per kg body-weight)
5–12 days	145 (105–195)
12–28 days	200 (170–225)
1–2 months	190 (160–220)
2–3 months	175 (145–200)
3–4 months	160 (130–180)
4–5 months	150 (130–170)

MILK DRINKS

If I drink a good deal of milk will I produce more breast milk?

Probably not. Cow's milk provides the additional energy (calories)
and protein you need to lactate efficiently, but so do other foods.
Provided you eat a nutritious diet, you don't have to drink extra
milk to produce more milk.

Among poorly nourished women in the developing nations the
situation is rather more complex. Although these women usually
produce adequate supplies of milk even when their diet is poor, they
are able to produce more milk if they obtain extra nourishment.
This is the basis of the concept 'feed the mother and thereby the
infant'.

MILK INTAKE: SELF-REGULATION

*Why is it that breast-fed babies tend to be less chubby than bottle-fed
babies?*

At first thought it might seem that mothers using formula feeds
either prepare the mixture wrongly so that it is too strong and contains an excess of energy, or that they force feed their babies. This is

probably not the answer, and the reason may be because of the composition of human milk.

Human milk changes in composition during the feed. The first milk to be sucked contains 1 to 2g less fat than the rest of the milk (the hindmilk). During the day the fat content of human milk varies. It reaches a peak in the late morning, and most of the extra fat occurs in the hindmilk. If a mother's 'let-down' reflex is working efficiently, she will be able to make more hindmilk, which contains more fat, available for her baby, and so give him a greater supply of energy than if she gives him a bottle. Hindmilk has a different taste from foremilk. This may be the factor which prevents most breast-fed babies from overeating. Doctors working in Oxford have observed that breast-fed babies have 'powerful self-regulatory controls' to overeating, which are not found in bottle-fed babies. They also observe that as different babies want different amounts of milk, the 'individual infant's needs would be best met if he is allowed to take what he wishes, preferably from his mother only'.

In other words, a breast-fed baby has a self-regulatory mechanism which controls his weight gain and prevents him becoming obese. This self-regulatory ability which enables the baby to take as much breast milk as he wants, and no more, may be related to the altered composition of the fat content and to the taste of hindmilk.

The self-regulatory mechanism may not operate in all breast-fed babies, and some do become overweight. However, by the time they are three or four years old most have lost the excess and returned to a normal weight.

MILK: OVERSUPPLY

I have an oversupply of milk. It annoys me that milk leaks out of my other nipple between feeds, making damp stains on my clothes. Once or twice when feeding my baby he has begun to splutter and I'm afraid of him inhaling the milk into his lungs. What can I do?

Leaking of breast milk between feeds means that your 'let-down' reflex is working well. In time, supply and demand adjust; meanwhile obtain (or make) some absorbent nursing pads, which you can put in your bra over your nipples. An old mum's trick to stop the 'let-down' leakage is to put the pad of your hand over the nipple and to press firmly. If the other breast leaks when you are feeding, let the milk drip into a small towel or into a small mug. Don't leave your breast covered or the nipple may get 'soggy' and is more likely to be damaged when the baby feeds from that side.

Don't cut down your food or liquid intake to stop the leak. It is unnecessary and doesn't help. Another folk belief also is not true: that if you leak you won't have enough milk for the baby when feeding time arrives.

The worry about too much milk causing the baby to choke and splutter is real. One way of coping with this is by posture feeding. The Nursing Mothers' Association of Australia suggests the following method.

Posture feeding

Possibly the most effective way to cope with spraying milk and a choking baby is to posture feed – to feed lying down with your baby on top of you. It is surprisingly comfortable and effective once you

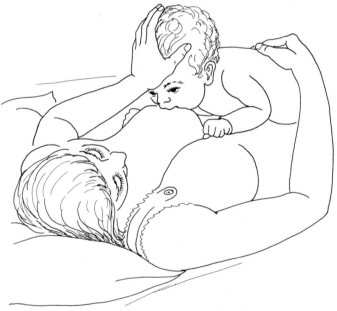

Fig. 30   Posture feeding

have mastered it. The secret is in the correct placing of your hand on the baby's forehead, with your elbow taking the weight (Fig. 30).

You lie on your back, on the bed, sofa or even on the floor, with a pillow or two under your head and a towel or nappy under your back to catch the dribbles of milk. Pull the baby gently up to one breast, with his body lying across yours and support his forehead with the heel of your hand, positioning your elbow on the bed, sofa or floor to take the weight of his head. Your left hand will support his head when he is feeding from the left breast, right hand for right breast. Don't try to support him by his shoulders as his head will drop down and his nose will become buried in your breast.

You may be able to manage to feed, and supervise your toddler at the same time if he or she joins you on the bed for a little rest too. Getting up during feeds is more troublesome than with a normal sitting position, but it's very good for your tummy muscles. The baby may still splutter occasionally during posture feeding, but being on his stomach he will recover more easily and so frighten himself, and you, less severely. As spraying and fullness decrease to manageable proportions you will be able to stop posture feeding, or just begin the feed this way and then finish the feed in the normal feeding position.

Most mothers find they only need to posture feed for the early morning feed, or for the first few minutes of any feed when the milk is flowing fast. In some cases a mother finds it is necessary for her baby to finish the feed in the normal position for him to sufficiently empty the breasts. An alternative method of posture feeding is to prop up the young baby with pillows on his mother's lap so that he has to 'suck uphill'. An older baby can suck this way by sitting up on his mother's lap.

MILK PRODUCTION: IS IT ADEQUATE?

Does an average mother produce enough milk each day to breast feed her baby for six months?

Breast feeding creates a situation of supply and demand: the amount of milk secreted by the mother adjusts to meet the baby's demands. Breast milk provides about 70kcal(293.3kJ)per ml but the variation between feeds is considerable.

The average milk output of mother's breast milk per day has been calculated for two groups of healthy Swedish mothers by test-weighing babies before and after feeds (Fig.31). A problem in using test-weighing is that the smooth rhythm of feeds may be upset by the method and both the prolactin and 'let-down' reflexes may be impaired. This would lead to an underestimate of the amount of milk produced. The investigation of a small number of babies using a new method, in which the baby was given a small dose of 'heavy water' by mouth, showed that the babies obtained a larger amount of milk than test-weighing indicated. The babies were aged two to four months old, and obtained more than 1000ml in most cases, compared with around 800ml obtained by test-weighing. A study in Perth, Western Australia, of healthy breast-feeding women whose babies were between one and six months of age has also shown that milk production averaged well over 1000ml.

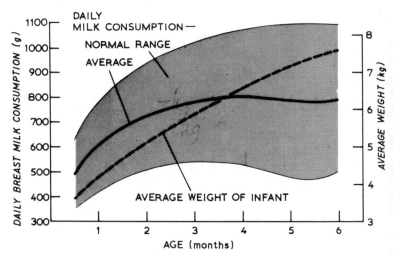

Fig. 31   Breast milk consumption (daily) of healthy full term infants, and their average weights, for the first six months of life. (The average milk consumption, and the upper and lower limits of its normal variations are shown)

These findings, if confirmed by other studies, are important as they indicate that most women in the developed nations, and the affluent 10 per cent of women in the developing nations, can exclusively breast feed for at least six months if they wish to without affecting the normal growth rate of their baby.

The situation among some poorer women in certain developing nations is less favourable. Studies in the Gambia and other countries indicate that a number of women living in urban slums and in the rural areas are only able to secrete sufficient milk for the baby's needs for the first three months of its life. This is because the women have chronic malnutrition, due to an inadequate intake of energy. The additional burden of pregnancy increases their energy deficit, so that they are unable to lay down fat stores during pregnancy. This means that they have no stores available to provide the extra energy needed to secrete breast milk, with the result that milk production declines and becomes insufficient for the baby when it is two or three months old. The babies are hungry, fail to gain weight and are given supplementary feeds of pap, made with contaminated water, or of sweetened condensed milk, excessively diluted. The result is infant malnutrition and a death rate which may reach 50 per cent.

The solution to this socio-medical problem is less easy. The women could be provided with formula milk, bottles and teats, at a price they could afford (which is very little), if the scheme was paid for by the government. A more appropriate solution is based on the axiom that it is better to feed the mother and hence the child, via breast milk, rather than to concentrate on giving the baby supplementary milk products. Most experts have interpreted this philosophy as needing to give the lactating mother supplementary foods, but such intervention has not led to a significant increase in milk production. The reason is that the extra foods had been used by the mother to restore her own depleted tissues rather than to provide energy for additional milk secretion.

The problem is likely to be solved if food supplements are given to each pregnant woman from early in pregnancy and are continued throughout the time she lactates. In many countries this means that food supplements will be needed throughout a woman's reproductive years. If a mother is given these food supplements she should be able to feed her baby exclusively on breast milk for four to six months without the need to supplement its diet with pap, condensed or formula milk. The food supplements in pregnancy permit the woman to lay down fat stores from which energy for milk secretion can be released when needed; the food supplements during lactation provide the energy needed to make up that released from fat stores to provide the 500kcal(2095kJ) required each day for adequate milk secretion.

MILK PRODUCTION AND PARITY

Does it make any difference to the quantity of milk produced if it is a first or a later baby?

The quantity of milk produced depends on the efficiency of the prolactin reflex and the 'let-down' reflex. In theory, a mother feeding her first baby is more tense and so inhibits the reflexes more easily. In practice this doesn't happen.

Provided the mother is confident about her ability to breast feed, is motivated to feed and feeds her baby on demand, there is no difference in the quantity of milk she produces.

MILK SUPPLY: HOW TO IMPROVE

Will any drug improve my milk supply?

The milk supply depends on adequate, frequent suckling to induce prolactin release, and a relaxed confident mother to ensure that the 'let-down' reflex operates efficiently. A poor milk supply may be due to insufficient milk production, consequent upon an inadequate prolactin release. More often it is due to an inefficient 'let-down' of milk.

You will improve your milk supply if you feed your baby when the baby wants to be fed and for as long as he wants to suckle. This means that unless your baby is hungry, he won't suckle strongly. When your baby is hungry and cries, feed him, and let him suckle as long as he wants on each breast. Some authorities also suggest adding extra feeds even when your baby doesn't ask: but the validity of this advice is doubtful.

You will improve your milk supply if you are relaxed and confident about your ability to breast feed. It is now known that emotions can affect the amount of prolactin released. If you are tense, hurried, or overtired you may reduce your prolactin release, and consequently make less milk. To avoid this, plan your day, cut out the inessentials (like keeping the house spotless!), get your partner to help with the housework and cooking, decide who you want to see and tell the others to call again.

All kinds of magic, ceremonies, ritual and drugs have been used by women to improve the milk supply. In primitive societies some women wear charms depicting big breasts. In modern societies, in Europe, stout has a reputation for inducing milk flow, presumably because of its 'milky' foam. These methods work by reducing a woman's anxiety that she has enough milk, and by releasing the inhibition anxiety places on the 'let-down' reflex.

A few women fail to obtain a good release of prolactin in spite of frequent suckling; in a few others the baby seems not to suckle strongly. These women will obtain a better milk supply if they are given drugs which are known to induce an increase in the release of prolactin. One drug is called metoclopramide and is given as a capsule twice daily for two to four weeks, or until the baby's suckling improves the prolactin reflex.

If a woman has a history of lactation problems with a previous baby, or if her baby is unable to suckle and hand-expression of the breasts (or the use of a breast pump) fails to obtain a good milk supply, the use of metoclopramide may be indicated.

Most women who complain of insufficient milk are secreting the milk adequately but have a poor 'let-down' reflex. The advice given to improve your milk supply applies equally if you want to improve your 'let-down' reflex. You need to be calm, confident, unhurried, relaxed and to enjoy breast feeding. You need to cut out the inessentials and expect your partner to help with the household chores. You need to avoid being overtired (if you can) by having extra naps during the day. As well as this general advice, you can condition your 'let-down' reflex to operate more efficiently by feeding the baby regularly, by feeding at night, and by avoiding missing out feeds. Above all you need to remain confident about your ability to breast feed, despite conflicting advice (given by well-meaning relatives and friends and by clinic staff). You must remember that a baby wants different amounts at different times (just as you do!), and does not usually drink the same amount of milk each feed. Sometimes you have more milk than your baby needs; at other times your baby may need more than you have at that feed, but you can make it up the next feed.

A drug is available which may help your 'let-down' reflex become more efficient. It is Syntocinon nasal spray. Syntocinon is synthetic oxytocin and has the effect of that hormone. It is used once in each nostril before a feed and will help to improve your 'let-down' reflex if the other methods fail. You should only use the spray for as short a time as is necessary to get more milk – and more confidence in your ability to breast feed. Conversely, a quick way of reducing your milk supply and reducing your 'let-down' reflex is to give your baby complementary feeds. If you do this, he will suckle less vigorously and for shorter periods, both of which will reduce prolactin release and discourage the 'let-down' reflex.

NAPKIN RASH

My baby has developed a napkin rash, what shall I do about it?

A baby's skin is sensitive to irritation, whether that occurs from loose stools or from ammoniacal dermatitis. In the napkin area, the irritation is aggravated by the nappy. Breast-fed babies are less likely to develop napkin rashes than bottle-fed babies.

Napkin rashes are of several kinds and are usually due to the fact that the baby is overfed, which may give rise to an irritant dermatitis. An overfed baby often has loose stools, because of the speed with which the faeces pass through his gut following the stimulus of over-

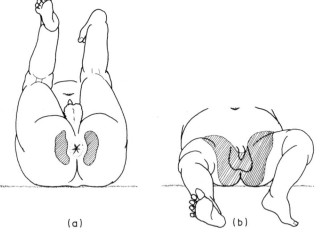

(a)   (b)

Fig. 32   Napkin rashes. (a) Sore buttocks from fatty diarrhoea;
(b) Ammoniacal nappy rash

feeding. The stools contain more fat than usual, especially if the baby has been fed on a full-cream formula milk. Irritant dermatitis, due to loose stools, is generally confined to the area between the cleft of the baby's buttock and the back of his scrotum if he is a boy (Fig. 32(a)). The treatment of napkin rash due to loose stools is to reduce the fatty diarrhoea by changing his diet, to change his nappies frequently, and to protect his skin with frequent applications of a greasy preparation.

Ammoniacal nappy rash

A more widespread napkin rash is caused by ammonia. Ammoniacal nappy rash is the most common form of nappy rash. It is produced by fermentation of a substance called urea (which is found in urine) by bacteria. Most of the bacteria come from the stools, so that ammoniacal dermatitis is more common among babies who have loose stools. When the baby passes urine, it wets the napkin, and the bacteria from the stool begin fermenting the urea, to produce ammonia. This is encouraged by heat, so that babies who wear waterproof pants, enclosing the napkin, are more likely to develop ammoniacal napkin rash.

A mother can often diagnose the rash by noticing that the nappy which has been on the baby all night has a strong 'fishy' smell.

If she notices this she can take action before the rash develops and becomes widespread. If it does it may cover the buttocks, the genitals, the upper thighs and the abdominal wall (Fig. 32 (b)). Oddly, the cleft between the buttocks is often not affected. The skin is red and sore, and may look wrinkled and 'papery'. Small blisters may dot the area, and some of them may be rubbed, causing ulcers.

Treatment is to prevent fermentation in the nappy. This is done by incorporating an antiseptic in the nappy which will kill the bacteria before they can act on the urine. The mother should wash the nappies in pure soap because detergents and enzyme powders may cause skin irritation if any traces remain on the nappy. With the last rinse add a mild antiseptic or dilute vinegar in a proportion of 30ml to 6 litres of water (one fluid ounce to a gallon).

In addition, the baby's skin needs to be covered with a cream containing petroleum jelly, zinc and castor oil.

Finally, when the rash is widespread, it is better to avoid wrapping the nappy around the baby. Instead let him lie on it for most of the day until the rash has healed. At night, or if you go out, you can put on a nappy in the usual way.

Thrush nappy rash (candida)

If the baby has thrush in its mouth, it is likely to have the fungus, called candida, in its stools, and this can cause a nappy rash. As well, thrush may infect an ammoniacal nappy rash. Thrush is caused by candida (monilia) and usually leads to small pimples and ulcers.

If you think your baby has thrush dermatitis, look in his mouth to see if there are any white patches. You would also be wise to visit your doctor. He will check if the baby has thrush and prescribe a cream or ointment containing nystatin, which you apply several times a day to the buttocks.

The prevention of nappy rash

1. Change the nappy often.
2. When soiled, wash the re-usable nappies in cold water and drop into a bucket containing hypochlorite disinfectant.
3. Do not use commercial detergents to wash nappies – use soap powders. If you wish you can add a mild antiseptic for the final nappy wash.
4. Clean the baby's skin when you change his nappy, and use oil or baby lotion if his bottom appears sore.
5. Avoid plastic pants when possible: if protection is wanted use disposable one-way nappy liners, such as Bubba-Dry, flannel pilchers or woollen pants.
6. If an ointment is chosen, one containing silicone may be helpful, but silicone must not be used if the skin is inflamed or abraded, as it prevents drainage.

The treatment of nappy rash

1. Change wet nappies frequently.
2. Clean and dry the nappy area carefully.
3. Expose the nappy area to the air for as long as practicable.
4. In mild cases, rub in a small amount of an ointment containing white soft paraffin, which will protect the skin, or an ointment containing petroleum jelly, castor oil and zinc.
5. If the skin is macerated and soggy, use a *cream* not an ointment.

6. Avoid folk remedies, such as application of fresh egg – which may cause skin sensitization; ointments containing mercury, which may cause toxicity; zinc oxide, *unless* it is dispersed in light paraffin – as it may dry the skin too much; talc, because it can cause damage to the macerated skin; and silicone, if the skin is inflamed or abraded, as it interferes with the drainage from the damaged skin surfaces.

7. If the baby has a secondary infection with candida, use nystatin ointment in addition to the other measures.

NIGHT FEEDS

Should I feed my baby at night, or let him cry?

The proportions of nutrients in human milk (and in cow's milk) suggest that human babies (and calves) are continuous feeders. If you watch a cow with a calf you will see that, apart from the time when she hides it so that it can sleep, the calf follows her about, feeding when it wants. Human babies cannot follow their mothers about, but they can let the mother know that they want to feed. Babies are not made to fit into a pattern devised more for the convenience of hospitals and mothers, although some do. Most babies do not sleep for a longer stretch than four or five hours. If that happens at night, the mother is lucky. Sometimes it does, but often it doesn't, and night feeds become necessary.

Night feeds may disturb the mother's sleep, but they are sensible. Milk production goes on 24 hours a day, and if your breasts become full and tense during the night you will wake, even if the baby doesn't, although once lactation is established, supply adjusts quite quickly and the discomfort ceases.

You don't need to wake your baby for a night feed, but if he wakes you should feed him. He can snuggle alongside you and feed from your breasts while you doze. In many cultures the baby sleeps in the same bed as his mother; he feeds when he wants to, often only partly waking up the mother.

It is impossible to say how long night feeds will go on. It depends on the baby. Some babies sleep all night from the time they are a month old; other babies continue to wake during the night up to the age of two or more.

Studies have shown that by three months of age, only one baby in two sleeps all night; by six months, seven out of 10 babies sleep all night and by nine months of age, nine out of 10 babies sleep all night.

Many parents find that night feeds are easiest if they have the baby in bed with them all night. When he wakes, all the mother has to do is to turn and offer him her nipple so that he can suckle. She does not need to worry that she will lie on him. Many thousands of women have their babies in bed all night, and none has been known to 'over-lie' the baby. They would both wake up before it happened.

NIPPLE DISCHARGE

I am pregnant and have developed a brownish discharge from my nipple: is this serious?

A few women develop a reddish, brown or chocolate discharge from one or both nipples during late pregnancy or in the first days after childbirth. If the latter occurs the colostrum may be discoloured. In a few cases the discharge appears some months after birth.

The cause of the condition generally is unknown although, rarely, trauma may be a cause. It is not likely to be due to breast disease. If the discharge occurs in pregnancy the woman should stop breast expression (if she is doing this), and if the discharge persists for about four weeks she should visit her doctor, so that he may examine her breasts and reassure her that she has no breast disease.

NIPPLES: FLAT

My nipples were rather flat in pregnancy and although I drew them out as recommended they haven't improved much. Will I be able to breast feed?

In all probability you will, as the nipples become more protractile with suckling. You should continue to draw out your nipples (see p. 43), and may find it helpful to wear breast shields for an hour or so before you feed. This helps to make the nipples more erect and easier to get deep into the baby's mouth. Some authorities suggest you use a breast pump if you have this problem; the cheap suction pump is quite adequate, although, as noted on page 108, this pump is not very useful when dealing with engorged breasts.

NIPPLES: SORE

What can I do about sore or blistered nipples? I am very anxious as I had a lot of trouble with my nipples when I breast fed my first baby.

Research has shown that sensitivity of the nipple varies during the menstrual cycle, is reduced during pregnancy and greatly increases within a few hours of childbirth.

Many women complain that their nipples are sensitive (sometimes painful) in the first days of breast feeding. A few women develop a painful blister or crack on the surface of the nipple.

The problem of sore nipples can be minimized if nursing mothers take some precautions.

Prevention of nipple soreness

1. Keep your nipples dry and expose them to the air as much as you can, either by leaving your bra open, or by inserting tea strainers (cut off the handle!) under your bra to stop the bra or your clothing rubbing your nipples.

2. Some mothers find comfort by using a nipple shield which prevents direct suction on the nipple. Before you put a nipple shield on your nipple, express a little milk into it to encourage your baby to suck at the teat.

3. Do not apply anything which will harden or dry your nipples. The surface skin is sensitive and shouldn't be made leathery. Avoid methylated spirits, Tinct. Benz. Co. BPC, mercurochrome and iodine.

4. Make sure that your nipple is well inside your baby's mouth so that he does not 'chew' the nipple (p. 48). Also make sure that he can breathe easily (p. 45). If he cannot he will 'fight' at your breast and in doing so your nipple may, to some extent, slip out of his mouth so that he chews on the nipple itself.

Treatment of sore nipples

Before feeding

1. Relax before you feed, be unhurried and deliberate.

2. Express a little milk on to the surface of your nipple so it slides easily into your baby's mouth.

3. If your breasts are very full, hand-express some milk so that your baby can get the nipple well inside its mouth.

4. If the pain is bad, you can take a mild painkiller with safety.

When feeding

1. Feed more often, for shorter periods.

2. Always start on the least sore side, and change sides once or twice during the feed to give your nipple a rest.

3. Make sure that your baby can breathe easily when he sucks at your nipple. You can be sure of this if you position yourself comfortably and, supporting your baby in the bend of your arm, make sure his nose is free, his chin against your breast. If he can't breathe easily, he will pull back and suck on your nipple instead of holding it deep inside his mouth. If the baby does this you will feel pain, particularly when he first sucks, and although the pain diminishes as the feed progresses, your nipple is being damaged.

4. Make sure that your nipple is well inside the baby's mouth so that his gums don't bite on the sore spot – in other words, make sure that your baby is correctly positioned (see p. 45).

5. When you take the baby off the breast, first break the suction (see p. 50).

After feeding

1. Dry the nipple carefully.

2. Rub a little anhydrous lanolin (wool fat) into the nipple.

3. Make sure the nursing pads and bra are perfectly dry before you dress. Excess moisture makes the nipple more sensitive and prevents cracks from healing. Don't use plastic-backed nursing pads as they hold moisture against the nipple.

NIPPLES: CRACKED

I have cracked nipples, what can I do about them?

The following measures usually help to relieve the pain and permit the woman to continue breast feeding.

● Apply a small amount of an antiseptic ointment or cream to the nipple before feeds at the first sign of a crack (e.g. Massé cream, Neotracin dusting powder, Savlon cream).

- Some paediatricians recommend the use of a McCarthy Mexican Hat or a thin latex nipple shield. The thin latex is made of soft plastic for the part which covers the areola and firmer plastic for the nipple extension. When the baby suckles he draws the nipple into the extension (by negative pressure) but because of the firmer plastic suckling is not painful.

- Usually the use of the nipple shield is sufficient to relieve the pain and to enable feeding to continue. Sometimes, as a last resort, it may be necessary to take the baby from the breast completely for 24 hours or until the crack or blister has healed. If healing is slow, consult your doctor.

- Hand-express the milk and feed this to your baby by dropper, spoon or bottle.

- Treat the nipple as described earlier.

- Restart feeding from the affected nipple very slowly to get it back to working condition, e.g. first day – one feed; second day – two feeds 12 hours apart; third day – three feeds eight hours apart, and so on until you are again fully breast feeding. Look carefully at the nipple after each feed. If it does not continue to heal you may have to restart feeding even more slowly, with just a few minutes instead of a full feed to begin with.

  During this re-introduction, continue to treat the affected nipple and to express and feed the expressed milk to your baby for the other feeds.

NUTRITION AND BREAST FEEDING

Do I need to eat extra food during pregnancy and when I breast feed?

The extra energy demand during pregnancy due to the growth of the baby, of the mother's uterus and breasts, and the increase in her blood volume, amount to about 150kcal(628.5kJ) a day. This is easily met by the energy provided in the diet a healthy, well-nourished woman usually eats.

During pregnancy and when breast feeding a mother does not need to 'eat for two' although she has to provide her fetus or baby with all his nourishment. She should eat a balanced nutritious diet, and largely avoid carbohydrate-rich 'junk foods'. Each day she should try to eat lean meat or poultry or fish or eggs. Each day she should eat some fresh fruit and vegetables. As well she should drink at least 500ml of milk (or use it in cooking) or, if she prefers, eat 60g of cheese each day. She may eat bread, but should limit her intake to between four and six slices and should choose wholemeal bread preferably. She should also limit the amount of sugar she takes. If she eats a nutritious diet during pregnancy which provides about 2400kcal(10 056kJ) of energy she will gain between 9 and 14kg of which 4kg is fat. This fat is available to provide energy during lactation and provides over 30 000kcal(125 700kJ) of energy. The energy cost of lactation is about 500kcal(2095kJ) a day. If the energy stored in fat is released over a five-month period it provides 200kcal(838kJ) of energy each day. This leaves an energy deficit of 300kcal(1257kJ). The diet eaten by most women in Western countries provides over 2400kcal(10 056kJ) and as the energy needs of these women for body functions and daily activity are about 2000kcal(8380kJ), a well-nourished woman does not need to eat extra food when breast feeding. But if she is anxious, all she has to do is to eat an extra slice of wholemeal bread with butter and cheese, each day. This will easily provide the extra calories needed for lactation.

OVERFEEDING

I am breast feeding. Can I overfeed my baby?

It is very difficult to overfeed a breast-fed baby as he tends to regulate his own supply (see p. 128). If he 'possets' after a feed, it does not mean he is being overfed, it shows he has had enough. Overfeeding occurs almost exclusively among bottle-fed babies, usually because the baby is given a formula which has been made too strong, or contains too much fat or too much salt (see p. 116). Overfeeding among bottle-fed babies causes vomiting and diarrhoea. After a feed the baby regurgitates or vomits a large amount of milk, and passes large, loose, smelly stools several times each day. He cries between feeds and is unhappy. Often he develops a napkin rash, especially in the cleft between his buttocks.

The treatment is obvious. Overfeeding is prevented if the baby is breast fed. It is eliminated among bottle-fed babies if less food is given, or if a change is made from full-cream milk to a half-cream milk.

PESTICIDES IN BREAST MILK

I am worried about the effect of pesticides in human milk. Can anything be done?

It is true that certain pesticides are found in breast milk, and this is sometimes given as a reason for changing to formula feeding. Cow's milk also contains pesticides, but as the formula is prepared by the infant-food manufacturers from the milk of many cows grazing in different localities the amount of pesticide contamination is reduced.

In several countries, including Australia, pesticide levels in human milk are declining so that, in general, lactating mothers need not be concerned about pesticides in breast milk.

PREMATURE BABIES: BREAST FEEDING

Is it possible to breast feed a premature baby?

Premature or low-birth-weight babies are of two kinds. The first are babies who were born before term (preterm babies) usually defined as before the end of the 37th week of pregnancy. The second are those babies who are born at or near term but are 'small for dates'.

The problems the babies have in adapting to life are not identical, but both kinds of baby thrive best on breast milk.

If you have a low-birth-weight baby (this is the preferred word for the two groups), he may need to be treated in an intensive baby-care nursery at least for the first few days of his life.

In the past, everybody except the staff were rigorously excluded from these nurseries, as it was believed that visitors (including the baby's mother) introduced infection. Twenty-five years ago, in Malaya, we found that was not true and we encouraged mothers to help care for their babies. Today, most paediatricians encourage mothers to visit their small babies in the nursery and to become involved in their care.

Most paediatricians now visit the mother as soon as possible after the baby is born, and before she comes to see him in the nursery. The paediatrician explains to her that her baby may look 'scrawny' (unlike the idealized picture she may have formed), and will be in an incubator. He will explain why the baby is connected by wires and tubes to machines. He will explain that the baby will be naked, except for a nappy, but that the temperature and oxygen of the incubator is controlled (a bit like in a space capsule) so the baby won't get cold. He will mention that the baby may appear to be fighting for breath.

When the mother visits her baby for the first time, she may find it easier if she is able to talk with the nurses who are caring for her baby. She should feel free to ask any questions which worry her. It is also easier if the baby's father joins her for the first visit. It is important that she visits her baby and cares for him as much as she can, because this will help her to 'bond' with him and may stimulate her prolactin and 'let-down' reflexes. As soon as it is appropriate, most paediatricians encourage mothers to touch the baby by inserting a hand through one of the 'ports' of the incubators.

If the mother hasn't been prepared, the first visit may be quite distressing, particularly if the mother didn't expect to see her baby in an incubator, connected by the wires which monitor its heart rate, its breathing, its blood oxygen and so on.

The mother's ability to provide breast milk will be increased if she has an active 'let-down' reflex. The 'let-down' reflex is stimulated by suckling, which is impossible in the case of a small preterm baby. Experiments in Denmark have shown that the 'let-down' reflex is enhanced if the woman uses an oxytocin nasal spray (once in each nostril) to induce an increase in lactation before using a breast pump. In the Danish study, women who used the spray between the second and fifth day after childbirth obtained two to three times the yield of milk, compared with women given a nasal spray which contained no oxytocin. The composition of the milk was unaltered, and the spray had no ill-effect on the mother or her baby.

In the early days of his life, the baby may have to be fed by an intragastric tube, because he cannot be relied on to swallow properly. The mother can provide the milk he needs by hand-expression, or by using a breast pump. The routine used varies between hospitals but in most the nursing staff, the paediatrician and the mother talk it over, so that the mother understands why a particular routine is used. If no one tells her, she should insist that she is given the opportunity to discuss the whole matter. This is important, because producing milk is the only way at this early stage of her baby's life that she can express her love for, and her concern about her baby. She should then take the expressed milk to the nursery and watch the baby being fed through the intragastric tube.

Once he is breathing properly and is ready to be taken out of his incubator, at least for a while, the mother is encouraged to cuddle and to care for him, and then, when he is ready, to feed him at her breast.

The early contact between the parents and their low-birth-weight baby is important for 'bonding' as Drs Klaus and Kennell have shown, and it encourages the milk flow.

It is also much more sensible than the older regimen which excluded mothers and fathers from touching their baby and only let them view the baby through a glass wall.

Very low-birth-weight babies

If your baby is very tiny, that is he has been born at least eight weeks preterm and weighs less than 1500g, additional problems arise.

Babies of this weight are unable to suckle at the breast because their suckling and swallowing mechanisms have not become sufficiently mature. As well, their digestive mechanisms are immature and fats and some sugars (especially lactose or milk sugar) are relatively poorly absorbed. The babies tend to be thin and have very limited fat stores so that they are poorly insulated.

In the past all these babies were fed, initially by tube, on formula milks. Some paediatricians now feed the tiny babies either intravenously (intravenous alimentation) or by tube using freshly expressed breast milk (FEBM). The reason for avoiding formula milk is that babies fed with formula milk seem more likely to develop a serious and often fatal bowel disease called necrotising enterocolitis.

The main problem in using FEBM is the difficulty in obtaining it in the days before the mother's milk is flowing freely. In some neonatal units other lactating mothers supply the FEBM; in others the collection of 'drip' breast milk has been established. It has been observed that between 15 and 20 per cent of women who have established lactation produce milk which drips from the opposite breast during breast feeding. The amount of 'drip' breast milk varies, but about 100ml is produced each day. The milk has to be collected, pooled, pasteurized and frozen and made available and this is expensive in time and money. The FEBM also has to be modified by adding protein, calcium, vitamin A and a small amount of sodium, because of the particular needs of the very small baby. For these reasons most paediatricians prefer to continue using formula milk until the baby weighs more than 1.5kg and the mother's milk is flowing easily.

PROJECTILE VOMITING

My baby is three weeks old and has begun vomiting after each feed. The vomit seems to shoot out of his mouth. Is this serious?

In a few babies – usually male – vomiting begins between two and four weeks after birth. At first the vomiting does not occur after every feed, and the baby is hungry and alert. The vomit rapidly becomes projectile. It occurs after each feed, and the baby begins to lose weight. The condition is due to a progressive narrowing of the pylorus (the part of the intestines just below the stomach). The condition is congenital, but at birth the pylorus is normal, the narrowing developing after birth. If a baby has projectile vomiting, a doctor should be consulted. If the baby has pyloric stenosis, surgery is needed to cure the condition.

REFUSING TO FEED

My baby is often restless and refuses my breast. Is he abnormal?

Some babies seem to be easily distracted when feeding, they are restless, 'fussy', will only suck for a short time and then stop. These behaviours may be very distressing to the mother and can lead to a lack of confidence in her ability to breast feed, with a reduction in the prolactin and 'let-down' reflexes and less milk.

The reasons for the baby's refusal to feed are often obscure, but the following suggestions may help:

- If you are tense your baby may notice it. Try to relax before and during the feed. You will have to find what helps you relax most. It may be deep breathing, having a shower, reading a magazine or just sitting, eyes closed, fantasizing.

- When you handle your baby keep calm, talk to him gently and feed him in a quiet area away from bright lights and other distractions.

- Check whether or not your breasts are overfull. If they are express a little milk before feeding so that your nipple and areola can be taken easily into your baby's mouth.

- Make sure that the baby is comfortable and can breathe when he suckles.

- If you have too fast a flow, so that the baby may feel he is choking, try posture feeding (see p. 130).

RE-LACTATION

I gave up breast feeding but now I would like to breast feed my baby. How can I do this?

There are several reasons given for wanting to breast feed after an interval when the baby has been given formula feeds from a bottle: (1) the baby may have been weaned early, and then the mother discovered that he was allergic to cow's milk; (2) the baby (or the mother) may have been in hospital because of illness or injury; (3) the baby may have been in an intensive neonatal care unit because its birth weight was low; or (4) in some cases, the mother misses the nurturing effect of breast feeding and wants to resume.

It is possible to re-establish lactation but the longer the interval between giving up breast feeding and the decision to re-lactate, the harder it is. The initial technique has been described on page 56. Once the baby is with the mother, frequent suckling is the key to re-lactation and encourages her confidence that she will succeed in re-establishing breast feeding. Until the milk supply is fully established, she will have to give the baby formula milk as well as breast milk or he will become frustrated and hungry. She should give him formula milk by bottle or spoon (which prevents him preferring the teat to the nipple) and then offering him the breast. If she wishes, she can use the Lact-Aid device (see p. 57) to give the baby the formula milk, so that he learns to accept the mother's nipple.

After the baby has finished feeding from the breast the mother should hand-express her breasts to encourage the prolactin reflex and promote milk secretion. This is also promoted by frequent suckling and, if possible, she should feed the baby every two hours. As her nipples may be tender, she should not let her baby suckle for too long. The length of time he suckles can be increased as the nipples become accustomed to the suckling.

Breast milk will begin to come in, rather slowly at first, but it will increase until in time – this may be as short as two weeks, or as long as six weeks – about one-quarter of re-lactating women achieve full breast feeding; others partially breast feed, needing to complement or to supplement the feeds. Not every woman is able to re-lactate so that a mother should not feel inadequate or guilty if she doesn't succeed.

Recently a drug, metoclopramide, has become available which helps to re-establish lactation. Metoclopramide is a potent stimulator of prolactin release. It is given eight-hourly for seven to ten days before starting re-lactation. In addition, the use of an oxytocin nasal spray just before breast feeding may increase the 'let-down' reflex.

RHESUS NEGATIVE MOTHER

I am Rhesus negative and have been told I have Rhesus antibodies. Is it safe for me to breast feed?

Some Rhesus antibodies are transferred from your blood to your breast milk. They will not affect your baby because they are eliminated in his intestines so that he will not absorb any.

You can breast feed your baby.

SALTY FOODS AND BREAST FEEDING

Is it possible that if I eat a lot of salt when breast feeding my baby will get a salt overload?

No, human milk, in contrast to cow's milk, has a low concentration of salt and other minerals. Cow's milk contains nearly six times as much phosphorus, nearly four times as much calcium and nearly four times as much sodium as human milk. The baby's kidneys have to handle this extra load, and sodium retention may occur. This makes the formula-fed baby thirsty: the mother gives more formula milk which increases the sodium load making it more thirsty. In rare cases the baby may get 'sodium poisoning'. This cannot happen to a breast-fed baby.

SEXUALITY AND BREAST FEEDING

What happens to a woman's sexual desire, response and enjoyment if she breast feeds?

For many women, breast feeding is a sexual experience. In most cultures the female breasts are perceived by most men, and by many women, as sexually arousing. Many women enjoy their breasts being fondled or sucked by their partner during sexual pleasuring.

After childbirth, women who choose to breast feed add a second function to their breasts, that of providing nourishment for the baby. This nutritional function may also produce sexual pleasure. The contact with the baby and its physical suckling stimulate many women sexually, some women lubricating vaginally and a few reaching orgasm during suckling. These two influences should increase a woman's sexuality during the time she breast feeds, but the evidence is that a woman's sexuality is very variable during lactation.

The reasons for this are not clear, but several suggestions have been made:

1. A woman who has been brought up to believe that her breasts must not be exposed and only touched by her husband may have inhibitions which will deter her from breast feeding. If she decides to breast feed she may feel guilty that her breasts are now exposed at intervals and have to be shared by her baby and her husband.

2. A woman who had difficulty in communicating with her partner about their sexual relationship may believe he is resentful that the baby has superseded him as the possessor of her breasts. The anxiety she feels about her partner's resentment may reduce her sexual desire and arousal.

3. Many women find adjustment to parenthood difficult. The incessant demands of the baby, the difficulty of feeling she has to be a super-mum, a super-housewife and a super-lover may leave the mother so exhausted that she is unable to respond to sexual advances. This in turn may make her feel guilty, as she no longer wants her partner to pleasure her sexually and finds it difficult to respond to him when he makes love to her.

4. The first attempt at sexual intercourse may be painful because of the episiotomy scar or because of vaginal irritation. This can lead to a fear of damage from sexual intercourse, and to an aversion to further sex.

In spite of these negative feelings about sexuality among women in the first weeks after childbirth, studies have shown that a majority have increased sexual desire, arousal and response. This enhanced sexuality is not related to the woman's age, nor to the number of children she has had, but mothers who breast feed are more likely to have increased sexuality after childbirth than mothers who bottle feed.

A woman's sexual response after childbirth is likely to be increased if, during pregnancy, she has talked with her partner about her sexual needs and preferences. During pregnancy the couple may have explored their feelings about sex, how they respond to touch, what kind of sexual pleasuring stimulates them most, and how they feel about the changing shape of the woman's body as pregnancy progresses. They may have talked about the man's feelings when the baby is born and he has to share his partner's breasts with their baby. Any possible resentment by the man will be minimized if he is able to fondle, touch and suck the woman's breasts during pregnancy, and is encouraged to continue this pleasuring when the baby has been born. Their sexual enjoyment will be helped as well if the man takes his share in parenting their baby.

SMOKING AND BREAST FEEDING

If I continue to smoke, will it reduce my breast milk?

There is now substantial evidence that cigarette smoking during pregnancy increases the chance of abortion occurring, increases the risk of haemorrhage during late pregnancy, reduces the birth weight of the baby and increases the death rate of newborn infants.

It remains to be determined if smoking is the cause of breast-feeding difficulties, or if the personality of a smoker leads to a disinclination to breast feed.

SOLIDS: EARLY INTRODUCTION

Why do some mothers give solids earlier than six months?

The main reason is fashion, which is supported by conflicting advice from friends, other mothers and, regrettably, the medical and nursing professions. This has led to a series of false beliefs about solids.

THE BELIEF	THE FACT
Solids help the baby sleep all night.	Babies given solids do not sleep any longer than babies given adequate milk feeds. In fact, solids may interfere with sleep if they are given too early in life when the baby's digestive system is not ready to digest the complex foods.
Solids make the baby more 'advanced'.	You are not in a chubby baby-making competition. Babies are individuals. Give your baby solids when he is ready – not to keep up with the Jones' baby.
The baby isn't gaining weight properly, so he requires solids.	Give him milk NOT solids.
The baby is always hungry.	Extra milk is more nutritious than solids which are usually 'complex carbohydrates'.
Breast milk isn't 'strong' enough.	Breast milk is always the correct strength.

SOLIDS: WHEN TO INTRODUCE

When should I start giving my baby solids?

Fashions change. Until the late 1940s, most paediatricians said that solids should not be given until the baby was at least nine months old, unless he was 'unsettled at night' when a mother might give some cereal. From the 1950s until about 1975, the trend was to give solids earlier in life. In the USA, a majority of infants are given solids (foods other than breast milk or formula milk) by two months of age. In Britain and Australia over half of mothers give their baby solids by three months of age. The introduction of solids so early seems due to aggressive marketing, to social pressures to have a 'chubby' baby, and to the erroneous belief that early solids will help the baby to sleep all night. Until recently these various pressures were not resisted by doctors, a majority of whom believed that solids should be introduced early.

It is now appreciated that the early introduction of solids is inadvisable for several reasons:

● Starting solids before four or six months of age may interfere with sound eating habits and encourage overfeeding. A breast- or formula-fed baby can stop sucking when he has had enough. A baby fed solids before the fifth month of life can't tell his mother that he doesn't want the food if she spoons it in. By five months he has developed sufficiently to indicate he would like food by leaning forward and opening his mouth, or, if he has had enough, by turning his head away. Until he can do this, to give him solids is to 'force feed' him like a Strasburg goose!

● Starting solids too early may lead to an excessive intake of calories, which is converted into fat, and of salt, which may make the baby thirsty. The mother then gives her baby more food so that he becomes fat.

Obesity in babies, due to overfeeding with incorrectly mixed formula feeds and the early addition of solid foods, is a factor which may lead to obesity in adult life, to an increased risk of high blood pressure and of heart attacks. A further disadvantage of starting solids early is that they may interfere with the absorption of iron from breast milk.

● Many mothers begin to give their babies solids early because they believe that the baby is hungry – in spite of being breast or bottle fed; or because of conflicting advice given by friends, health visitors and nurses or doctors; or because the mother believes the 'milk isn't good enough for the baby'. If a mother is breast feeding her milk is good enough but she may need to feed more frequently. Suckling encourages increased milk production by the release of more prolactin, and gives the baby more milk when he needs it.

Most doctors now recommend that the baby should not receive

solid foods until he is about five months old or more. First, this prevents the baby becoming obese. Second, it reduces the chance of the baby developing a 'milk allergy' to cow's milk, as this is used in most solids. Third, if you give solids too early you may reduce your milk supply, as the baby won't suckle so well. Fourth, solids, especially cereals, provide minimal nutritional benefit to the baby, as his intestinal enzymes are unable to digest cereals readily until he is about eight months old.

The time of starting solids depends on the individual baby because, like all humans, babies differ in their demands. The baby will generally let you know, by being restless and by wanting more than you can give him from your breasts. If he continues to be restless, unhappy and hungry for a few days, in spite of frequent feeds, you can assume he wants to start on solids, unless his restlessness is due to teething or a cold. If he starts reaching and putting things in his mouth, it is a further indication he is ready for solids. A good way of telling when solids are needed is when teeth appear. Most babies do not want solids until two teeth have appeared, and this is usually some time after six months of age. Teeth are generally an indication that the baby's digestive system has matured and that enzymes which break down complex foods are now being produced in the stomach and intestines.

The easiest way of finding out if your baby wants solids is to give him a small amount of the food you eat, from a spoon. You can mash vegetables or a banana, or cut meat finely, or give egg-yolk or stewed fruit and so save money. If you prefer, canned baby foods are available, but they are more expensive (if convenient) and, beware, some have extra salt and some extra sugar, so choose carefully. Using a spoon you need to put the food well back in his mouth, so that he can swallow it more easily until he has learned about eating from a spoon. The solid foods add extra nutrients (including iron if you give your baby meat) and provide variety.

If you find he doesn't want the solids you have given him, don't worry. Try something else another day. But your baby will still need, and want, your milk. You should continue giving him the pleasure of your breast until he is at least a year old, and able to take all foods from cup or spoon.

After a while he may want to have 'finger foods', that is food he can pick up, hold in his hand and eat – such as a crust, a rusk, or piece of meat.

It is important to make sure he has a milk feed first, as this is the main part of his diet. Gradually, as he learns to chew he will want more solids and less milk. By this time you can give a milk feed and solids alternately.

A good place to feed him is with you, at the family meal table, so that he can interact with the other members of the family.

SOLIDS: WHAT KIND

When I start giving my baby solids, which I don't intend to do until she is six months old, what kind of solids shall I give her?

Most nutritionists say that when mixed feeding is started, the baby should be given a variety of foods, and should not be fed entirely on commercial baby foods.

There are several methods of starting solids. One is to give the baby the food the family eats, appropriately minced, strained or mashed. The second is to buy commercially prepared baby foods which come in attractive tins. In the past, some of these foods contained an excessive amount of salt, and too much starch and sugar. Recent publicity has induced the baby-food manufacturers to eliminate the excesses and 're-formulate' their products, but the labelling of the cans showing the percentage of the contents is not sufficiently informative. The main problem about commercial baby foods, which are convenient, is that they cost between two and four times as much as the baby foods you can make at home.

Home-prepared baby foods are fresh and cheap. There are some points a mother should remember if she intends to prepare her own baby foods:

- Don't overcook the food.
- Steam, not boil, vegetables so that you don't lose the vitamins and minerals.
- Choose lean meat; boil it and skim off the fat before you mince it.
- Don't add salt or sugar, they are unnecessary and may induce bad eating habits in the baby.
- Avoid using canned fruits or vegetables as they are likely to contain added sugar or salt.

- Don't forget hygiene – clean utensils and hands when you prepare the food.

- Don't force your baby to finish the food if he doesn't want to, or you may overfeed him, and teach him to want to overeat.

In an article in *Choice*, the journal of the Australian Consumers' Association, the cost of commercial baby foods was compared with baby food prepared by the Association. The latter was always cheaper.

The following foods were suggested.

Beef and vegetable purée

Cover with water 450g of lean steak (lamb or mutton may be used instead) which has been minced.
Boil it, skim off any fat and pour off excess water.
Steam 400g potatoes, 300g carrots, 450g pumpkin.
Blend together the chosen meat and the vegetables.

Egg custard

Break a large grade (60g) egg* into ¾ cup milk and stir or blend.
Bake until set in an oven; or cook in a cup standing in a saucepan of water.
*(If the baby is under six months old, only the yolk should be used to avoid protein allergy.)

In planning your baby's diet, try to give him the experience of a variety of tastes.

Many mothers start with mashed banana, mashed buttered potato or egg-yolk. Later they add egg custard, vegetable or meat purée, minced meat, stewed mashed fruit, oatmeal porridge and bread and butter.

When the baby starts wanting to hold things, he can be given rusks or biscuits, or the leg bone (drumstick) of a cooked chicken to chew on (rather than a teething ring).

Many paediatricians suggest that when solids are introduced they should be given at feeding time, after the breast (or bottle) has been given. Small amounts (perhaps only a teaspoonful) are given initially; and the amount is increased as the days go by. New foods should be introduced one at a time, at intervals of a few days. As previously mentioned, if the baby doesn't like the taste do not persist, try again another day. Babies' tastes vary, some like sweet foods, some bland foods, and you have to take this into account.

SPORT AND BREAST FEEDING

I enjoy sport, can I take fairly strenuous exercise and breast feed?

If a lactating mother enjoys playing tennis, squash, golf, swimming, horse-riding or jogging, she can take part in these activities and can breast feed. She may find it more comfortable to wear a supporting bra and should make sure she replaces fluid lost by sweating. If she exercises vigorously, using up energy, she should increase her food intake. In spite of folklore, exercise by 'jolting the breasts' does not reduce milk secretion or cause milk in the alveoli-lobules to curdle.

STOOLS OF BREAST-FED BABIES

My breast-fed baby has a soft mustard-yellow stool. Is this normal?

Cow's milk curd differs considerably from human milk curd. Cow's milk curd is thick, tough and 'rubbery', although modern formula milks are modified to overcome this problem and to produce a less bulky dense curd. Human milk curd is soft and flocculent. Because of this, cow's milk curd usually passes through the baby's gut faster than human milk curd, but the reverse may occur. The curd may form an obstruction in the gut if the formula milk has not been diluted properly, and especially if the baby is small.

The stools of a breast-fed baby are soft, often unformed, not smelly and usually mustard yellow in colour, although occasionally they may be green. This does not indicate that the baby has a gut infection.

The frequency with which a breast-fed baby passes motions is very variable. Breast-fed babies sometimes go for two to seven days without a bowel movement. When the baby opens his bowels the stool may be large. This infrequency of bowel movements is normal, as breast milk is absorbed so well that there is little waste. The baby is not constipated unless the stool is hard and dry. It has nothing to do with the frequency of passing motions or with the baby 'straining to open its bowels'.

STRETCH MARKS

If I breast feed, will I get stretch marks on my breasts?

Stretch marks on the skin of the breasts, the abdomen, or the upper arms and thighs have the same origin. They are not caused by stretching but by local damage to the lower layers of the skin. This is associated with a temporary increase, in the blood of susceptible people, of glucocorticoid hormone produced by the adrenal gland. Stretch marks are common in Europeans and North Americans but unusual in Africans or Asians. The adrenal hormone is secreted in greater quantities in early adolescence, during pregnancy, in obesity and in certain diseases. What happens is that the hormone breaks down the collagen and elastic fibres in the skin, which heal leaving a pinkish line which fades to silver-white. Stretch marks are not caused by breast feeding, but by the changed hormonal environment of pregnancy. There is no treatment, nor can they be prevented by massaging oil into the breasts.

TEST-WEIGHING

I am given conflicting advice about 'test-weighing', who am I to believe?

Babies are individuals. They take in different amounts of food at different feeds. Sometimes they are hungry and sometimes they only want to suck at or play with the breast. It doesn't matter how much a baby gains in weight each week, as this will vary considerably.

Many small babies cry a good deal, but this is not abnormal and is not a sign that your baby is underfed, provided that his skin is elastic, his eyes are bright and his nappies are wet. Lack of weight gain and a crying baby do not indicate that he is getting too little food until it has persisted for several weeks. It means that he should be put to the breast more often, including night feeds.

In these situations, test-weighing is often advised by baby health nurses and doctors. Recent evidence confirms that, except in special cases, test-weighing the baby before and after feeding is a meddlesome, unscientific procedure which may cause unnecessary concern to the mother. It tends to make the mother anxious and so to reduce the efficiency of the 'let-down' reflex. Test-weighing should only be started after careful consideration and discussion and, if it is used, it must be made for every feed over a 24- or 48-hour period. This is the only way it is possible to establish how much milk the baby is obtaining.

TONGUE-TIE

I think that my baby is tongue-tied. Will this stop him breast feeding properly?

Parents often think that the baby is tongue-tied because his tongue seems to be tied to the floor of his mouth and he can't stick it out. It is normal for the 'tie' – the fold of skin which stretches from the tongue to the floor of the mouth – to vary in length between babies. During the first year of the baby's life the tip of the tongue grows, and the baby becomes able to stick out his tongue! Even if he doesn't it is of no importance as it causes no harm. It will interfere neither with feeding nor with speech. Most doctors now agree that tongue-tie is a normal variation which corrects itself in time.

Professor Illingworth, an eminent British paediatrician, wrote in 1979: 'Children can suffer much harm at the hands of doctors who do not know the normal, and normal variations do not require treatment. One has seen young babies operated on for tongue-tie, or cysts of the gum or palate, which disappear if left alone.'

Tongue-tie, if it exists, which is doubtful, will not prevent a baby breast feeding.

TWINS AND BREAST FEEDING

I am 24 weeks pregnant and I have been told by my doctor (who arranged for an ultrasound picture) that I will have twins. Is it possible for me to feed them?

Most mothers who have twins can feed them, because the breasts automatically supply the extra quantity of milk needed. Many mothers with twins prefer to feed them both simultaneously: the two babies suckling, one from each breast, each cuddled in the crook of their mother's arm (Fig. 33). Other women prefer to nurse each twin separately, as they claim they can devote more attention to the baby who is feeding. Each mother has to work out her own schedule, as the twins will not always wake up at the same time and the mother may not want to wake up the sleeping baby. If you choose to feed your twins at the same time, alternate your breasts so that the twin who sucks more strongly feeds from alternate breasts.

Twins are often born before term and have a low birth weight. The advantages of breast milk for such babies has been demonstrated quite clearly. Even if the smaller twin has to remain in the intensive-care nursery, most hospitals now encourage the mother to see the baby, and to touch and attend to it. If the baby is not fit to feed, you can express your breast milk and give it to him.

As a mother who is breast feeding twins needs to produce extra

Fig. 33   Breast feeding twins

milk, she should eat a nutritious diet, and cut down housework to a minimum. She has a full-time job looking after her babies!

UNDERFEEDING

Is it possible to underfeed a breast-fed baby?

A few breast-fed babies fail to thrive. They fall into two categories: fretful, underfed babies, and contented, underfed babies. Neither group is common, and most breast-fed babies thrive.

'Fretful' underfed babies: These cry a good deal and only feed for short periods before becoming irritable. They may vomit. They look undernourished. It is possible that inadequate milk supply is the cause or, if the mother has 'flat' nipples, the baby may not be able to suck properly. The mother may be tired and anxious, which reduces her 'let-down' reflex, and if the baby sucks poorly so that her breasts are not emptied, milk production will be diminished further.

The baby must be examined to make sure that he has no infection, especially thrush. The mother needs reassurance. She should make sure that her baby takes the whole of her nipple into its mouth, and should empty her breasts after each feed. In general she shouldn't suckle for more than 20 minutes, as her baby will become tired, but she should feed her baby more frequently.

If the baby is very fretful, her doctor may suggest a mild sedative such as chloral hydrate (30–60mg) given 10 minutes before a feed, although the use of this drug is controversial.

'Contented' underfed babies: These seem to suck well and to be satisfied after a feed. They sleep for long intervals between feeds, and often through the night. They look undernourished and fail to gain weight adequately. The reason for their contentment, despite undernourishment is not known.

Usually the mother only perceives that she has a problem when the baby is four to six weeks old, and she finds that his weight is still close to his birth weight. Panic results. The way to cope with the problem is to feed the baby at least every three hours during the day even if the mother has to wake him. Night feeds are less important, but the mother should offer the baby a feed when she goes to bed. If this doesn't lead to weight gain, it may be necessary to express the breast milk and to complement the baby's feeds. If the problem persists she should take her baby to a doctor. A mother who has this problem must not feel ashamed or guilty at her failure to breast feed. The problem lies with her baby – and doctors don't yet know why.

VITAMIN SUPPLEMENTS FOR BABIES

I have decided to breast feed my baby until he is at least six months old. Does he need to have vitamin supplements?

The baby of a woman who has been healthy and has eaten a balanced diet during pregnancy will start life with an adequate supply of most vitamins. Breast milk, from a healthy mother, contains sufficient vitamin A, thiamine (vitamin B_1), riboflavine (vitamin B_2), niacin, and pyridoxine (vitamin B_6). Unless the mother is a strict vegetarian (avoiding eggs as well as meat) her baby will get enough vitamin B_{12}. If she is a Vegan it is possible that her baby will become deficient in vitamin B_{12}, which may damage the development of its brain.

The only supplementary vitamins required are vitamin K and, in some countries, vitamin D. Vitamin C also needs to be considered.

Vitamin K

If the mother has eaten dark-green leafy vegetables in late pregnancy she should have provided her baby with adequate amounts of vitamin K, which he stores in his liver. The stored vitamin K is sufficient to protect the baby from haemorrhages until he starts synthesizing vitamin K in his intestines in the second week of life. In the first week his intestines are largely sterile as the bacteria have not yet multiplied in them, so that vitamin K synthesis cannot start.

If a baby lacks vitamin K, he is unable to synthesize the anti-bleeding substance prothrombin in his liver, and may develop haemorrhages. It is impossible to be sure if every baby has sufficient vitamin K in his body stores to prevent the development of haemorrhagic disease of the newborn, and most obstetricians recommend that all newborn babies are given an injection or a tablet of vitamin K soon after birth, so that haemorrhages are prevented.

Vitamin D (calciferol)

A baby needs about 400 international units of vitamin D to protect him against rickets. Breast milk contains only between 40 and 100 units in every litre (cow's milk contains half this amount), so that vitamin D deficiency may occur. However, humans have a way of avoiding vitamin D deficiency. Humans synthesize vitamin D in their skin if it is exposed to sunlight, so that if a breast-fed baby is exposed to the sun each day he will make enough vitamin D for his needs.

In cloudy, cold climates, it is probably wise to give a baby supplemental vitamin D, in a dose of 200 to 400 units each day. This dose should not be exceeded as the vitamin accumulates in body fat and may produce toxic effects.

Vitamin C (ascorbic acid)

A baby needs about 15mg a day of ascorbic acid. The breast milk-secreting cells actively concentrate ascorbic acid obtained from the mother's blood, so that the amount is higher than that in her blood. It averages 4mg per 100ml of breast milk. Provided a mother eats a diet containing fresh fruits and vegetables, supplements of ascorbic acid are unnecessary, but it is customary to give a baby vitamin C in the form of orange juice, tomato juice (two to four tablespoonfuls) or as a tablet, containing ascorbic acid – 25mg crushed in water and given from a spoon. Many mothers choose to give vitamin C syrup. This is particularly unsuitable as it is loaded with sugar and the stability of the vitamin C is in some doubt.

It might be thought that the babies of poorly-nourished mothers living in the developing nations need vitamin C supplements. In fact, most do not. If the baby is under six months of age, the mother needs food which will provide vitamins for her baby, rather than buying vitamin C tablets which are relatively expensive. From the age of six months babies can be given local fruits and vegetables which are available, cheap and contain vitamin C. These include dark-green leafy vegetables, sweet potato tops, pumpkin tops, papaya (paw-paw), and similar items.

VITAMINS FOR MOTHERS

When I breast feed do I need extra vitamins?

If you eat a nutritious diet, which includes meat, poultry or fish and fresh vegetables every day, and fresh fruit most days, it is unlikely that you will need extra vitamins for yourself. It is not certain whether your baby needs vitamins either, as some experts believe that the breast concentrates the vitamins you have in your body and this provides the baby with adequate supplies.

WEIGHT GAIN

How much is an average healthy baby expected to gain in the first year of his life? Should I be worried if my baby is not like the average?

Babies are individuals and gain weight at different rates. For convenience, doctors and other health professionals use charts which show expected weight gain of an 'average' baby. But remember, half

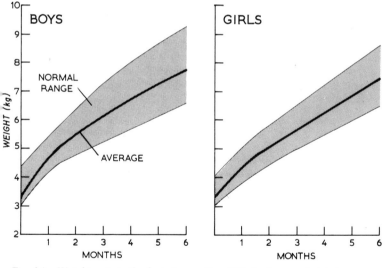

Fig. 34   Weight gain in the first six months of life for boys and girls (average and normal range in which 95 per cent of babies' weights will be found)

of babies may be expected to gain less than the average baby and half more. A better method of charting weight gain is to look at the rate of gain which 95 per cent of babies may expect (Fig. 34).

An average healthy baby (whatever an average baby is) may be expected to gain 150–200g(5½–7oz) a week in the first four months of life (that is after he has regained his birth weight). In the second four months he will gain 125–175g(4½–6oz) a week. In the third four-month period, the rate drops to 75–105g(2½–3¾oz) a week.

Another way of checking that your baby is gaining weight 'normally' is based on the observation that an average healthy baby, whatever his birth weight, may be expected to gain 3.5kg in the first five months of life and another 3.5kg in the next seven months. But it is quite normal for a baby to gain less than this. His activity, contentment and alertness are better guides to his progress than weight gain.

It is essential for the mother's peace of mind to remember that the baby's weekly or two-weekly weight gain will vary widely. The mother need only be anxious if her baby's weight gain is slow over several weeks, or if he shows other symptoms of distress, such as crying after feeds.

Many women choose or are advised to have their babies weighed at periodic intervals. A mother should avoid being preoccupied with the weight gain, as this is only one indication of his progress. Too many mothers are over-anxious about their baby's weight. A mother should also avoid comparing her baby's progress with the progress (as judged by weight gain) of the babies of her friends. Some babies gain quickly in the first few months of life (up to 400g a week for short periods), others gain weight slowly. A baby's development is better judged by his alertness, his energy, his appearance (bright eyes, elastic clear skin), and by his progress than by how much weight he has gained in the past one or two weeks.

If you want to weigh your baby for your 'Baby Book' that's fine, but don't be obsessed with his weight gain to the exclusion of the other, more important, measurements of his progress.

WEIGHT GAIN RELATED TO BABY'S AGE

I have heard that as a baby grows he needs less breast milk for his weight than in the early months of life?

A baby grows rather faster in the early months of its life than

later. An average baby may be expected to double his birth weight
in the first five months of his life, and to treble it in the next seven
months. This means that a baby weighing 3.5kg at birth, will weigh
about 7.0kg. at five months and about 10.5kg at one year of age. A
baby's weight gain over periods of a week or two weeks varies widely,
and a mother need only become anxious if the baby fails to gain
weight, or gains weight very slowly, over a period of several weeks.
As well, babies vary considerably in the amount of weight they gain,
and there is a wide range of normal.

An average baby needs about 150ml of milk for every kilogram he
weighs, but some babies like more and some less.

When a baby is breast fed, the amount of milk the mother supplies
increases up to about two months. At that time she secretes about
700ml of milk a day. From then on, the volume she produces depends
on how frequently she feeds. At five months she produces between
800 and 1200ml – her supply is adjusted to demand so a wide variation in the amount of milk produced is common.

The amount of milk per kilogram body-weight which a baby takes
therefore falls as he grows older, but the fat content of breast milk
increases so that he obtains all the energy and nutrients he needs.
You should remember that a breast-fed baby regulates his intake; he
decides his own needs and his intake does not depend on his weight.

WEIGHT GAIN ON COW'S MILK

*Friends have told me that when they switched from breast feeding to
bottle feeding the baby gained weight, does that make it sensible to
feed babies on cow's milk?*

This has been reported often. The rapid weight gain is due to
water retained because of the higher sodium content of many formula
milks. The baby weighs more, is chubbier but is not healthier; it is a
'wetter' but not a better baby.

WEIGHT GAIN: TEST-WEIGHING

How do I know if my baby is getting enough to eat?

Until recently many nurses expected babies to gain a precise
amount of weight each week, as if all babies behaved in the same

way. And of course they don't. Babies are as much individual as are adults: some put on weight quickly, some put on weight slowly.

Your baby is getting enough to eat if you feed him 'on demand' – that is his demand, not yours, and avoid feeding him to a rigid schedule. You can reassure yourself that he is thriving if he is a happy baby and if he has between six and eight wet nappies (diapers) each day. When this happens he is getting enough fluids. If you are breast feeding you are giving him enough nutrients and energy for health as well.

An objective way of telling if your baby is getting enough is to weigh him, but don't weigh him too often as you'll get confused and anxious as on some days babies gain weight and on others they don't. Even more anxiety-provoking is to weigh the baby before and after each feed. This is called test-weighing. If your baby hasn't taken what you believe (or have been told) he should at that particular feed, you'll get upset, and that will reduce your milk supply. Test-weighing should be reserved for sick babies and those who aren't thriving. Healthy babies take different amounts of milk at each feed. The baby knows better than you when he has had enough. If he hasn't had enough he will cry and ask for more, like Oliver! This means you will have to nurse him more often.

A few babies are sleepy babies. They sleep for four or five hours regularly. They sleep all night. When they ask for food they feed in a leisurely way and are not very demanding. In such cases it is probably helpful to have weekly weight checks, and if the baby's weight gain is poor you may have to coax him to wake up and to stay awake for longer.

But apart from sleepy babies, sick babies and those who obviously are not thriving, you need to weigh your baby only once every two weeks or thereabouts.

WITCHES' MILK

What is witches' milk?

After birth, the breasts enlarge in a number of babies and some of them produce a little milk. This is called witches' milk. It is due to the effects of the baby's own prolactin, or his own growth hormone acting on breasts which have been stimulated by the mother's sex hormones.

Witches' milk is of no importance; no treatment is required, the milk ceases and the breasts become flat after a few days or weeks.

WORK AND BREAST FEEDING

I am worried because I have read that if a mother leaves her baby to go to work it may suffer emotionally and physically. I have to go to work for financial reasons. Am I damaging my baby's development – and what can I do?

In many industrialized countries, over 25 per cent of mothers of babies, or of pre-school children, either choose to work or have to work to help to meet the financial commitments of the family.

A dilemma occurs because of the expressed view of many child psychologists that babies need the sustained presence of the mother to develop fully. This view is based on John Bowlby's work on 'attachment theory'. Attachment is a two-way process between mother and infant. It is, in fact, unrealistic to specify mother and infant, as attachment can, and does, occur between father and infant and other significant attachment-figures (such as a grandmother or, in certain social classes, a nanny) and the infant.

Attachment starts at about one month of life and persists until at least one year. (The interaction before this time is termed 'bonding'.) It has been shown that attachment is more secure if the mother responds rapidly and warmly to the baby's cues of crying and smiling, if she looks at and talks to him and cuddles him often. With the security of attachment the baby is more willing to explore his environment, distancing himself from his mother, but confident that she will be there when he returns. In contrast, less securely attached babies do not explore and are more dependent on the mother. It has been found that the more secure the attachment, the better is the child able to learn, to relate to others and to adjust to new situations, at least up to the age of three or four.

What then can be done to relieve any guilt a working mother may feel? An important point is that although the mother is usually the attachment-figure, other people can also become attachment-figures, provided that their numbers are few and that they are frequently in contact with the baby. This means that if a mother has to work but has a relative, such as her mother or a friend, who cares for and interacts with the baby (in other words becomes a 'surrogate mother'), the attachment-process should not be damaged.

Most women do not undertake paid employment outside the home until the baby is at least 12 weeks old, and many not until the baby is six months old, so the problem usually arises only after this time. Strategies can be developed to ensure that the optimum emotional, physical and nutritional needs of the baby are met when the mother has to work outside the home. The subject was discussed recently at a Joint WHO/UNICEF meeting on 'Infant and Young Child Feeding'.

Although the main discussions were about breast feeding, the necessity for many mothers to obtain paid employment outside the home was recognized and the meeting recommended that: 'Paid maternity leave of not less than three months postnatal, job security and economic support should be provided to all mothers whenever possible, and wherever possible, and the responsibility for economic support during maternity leave should be carried by the government, the industry in which the woman is working and international institutions.

'Crèches, paid breast-feeding breaks and other facilities should be provided wherever appropriate, in industry and in other relevant institutions, or close to the place of work to permit mothers to continue breast feeding and have close contact with their babies. Financing of crèches and other mechanisms that allow this continued contact of breast feeding should be carried by government and/or industry in which the mother is working.'

In spite of the clauses 'whenever possible', 'wherever possible', 'wherever appropriate' and the lack of firm evidence about the responsibility for financing the recommendations, the WHO/UNICEF statement is important.

The theory of attachment discussed earlier leads to the further recommendation that the crèches (or baby-care centres) are staffed by appropriately trained caretakers, who have the capacity to become attachment-figures for the baby during the period the mother is away.

If women exert pressure on society and on governments to provide these facilities; or if they can make their own arrangements within the community to establish crèches, and to obtain time to visit, play with, feed and cuddle their babies, two or more times during working hours, no reduction in the nutritional, emotional or physical development will occur among infants of working mothers.

References

The following references relate to comments and discussions within the content of the book and are given so that interested readers may be able to look them up. The page numbers refer to the text pages of this book.

(16) **Anatomy of the female breast:**
Applebaum, R. H. (1970). *Pediatric Clinics of North America*, **17,** 203.
Vorherr, H. (1974). *The Breast*. Academic Press, New York.

(20) **Changes in breast size and nipple sensitivity:**
Milligan, D. (1975). *British Medical Journal*, **4,** 494.

(21) **Changes in breasts in pregnancy:**
Vorherr, H. (1979). *Seminars in Perinatology*, **3,** 193.

(23) **Composition of human milk:**
Jenness, P. (1979). Review in *Seminars in Perinatology*, **3,** 275.

(23) **Benefits of breast milk:**
Berg, A. (1973). *The Nutrition Factor*. Brookings Institute, Washington.
Jelliffe, D. B. and Jelliffe, E. P. F. (1978). *Human Milk in the Modern World*. Oxford University Press, Oxford.
Waletzsky, L. R. (ed) (1979). *Symposium on Human Lactation*, pp. 79–5107. DHEW, Washington.

(26) **Breast feeding and bonding:**
Klaus, M. and Kennell, J. (1976). *Maternal Infant Bonding*. C. V. Mosby, St Louis.
Taylor, P. M. (ed) (1979). *Maternal-Infant Interactions. Seminars in Perinatology*, **3,** 1–103.

(30) **Physiology of lactation:**
Llewellyn-Jones, D. (1983). In *Clinical Reproductive Physiology*, (edited Shearman, R. P.). Churchill Livingstone, Edinburgh.

(60) **Breast augmentation:**
Reviews (1976). *Clinics in Plastic Surgery*, **3**, 167–233.

(61) **Breast cancer and pregnancy:**
Anderson, J. M. (1979). *British Medical Journal*, **1**, 1124.

(62) **Breast disease and the Pill:**
Vessey, M. P. et al (1972). *British Medical Journal*, **2**, 219.
Boston Collaborative Program (1973). *Lancet*, **1**, 1399.
Kay, C. (1981). *British Medical Journal*, **1**, 2089.

(70) **Breast feed, how long?:**
Waterlow, J. C. and Thomson, A. M. (1979). *Lancet*, **2**, 238–42.
Letters (1979). *Lancet*, **2**, 691 and 897.
Prentice, A. M. et al (1980). *Lancet*, **2**, 886–8.
Letters (1980). *Lancet*, **2**, 1306 and 1365.
Hitchcock, N. E. et al (1981). *Medical Journal of Australia*, **2**, 536–7.
Hitchcock, N. E. (1981). *Lancet*, **1**, 64.
Whitehead, R. G. and Paul, A. A. (1981). *Lancet*, **2**, 161–3.

(75) **Breast milk – anti-infective properties:**
Head, J. R. (1977). *Seminars in Perinatology*, **2**, 195.
Butler, J. E. (1979). *Seminars in Perinatology*, **3**, 255.
Editorial (1981). *Lancet*, **1**, 1192.

(76) **Breast milk banks:**
Department of Health and Social Security (UK) (1981). The collection and storage of human milk. *Rep Health Soc Sub no 22*. HMSO, London.
Letters (1982). *Lancet*, **1**, 284, 454, 568 and 569.

(88) **Breast feeding and coeliac disease:**
Littlewood, J. M. et al (1980). *Lancet*, **2**, 1359.

(90) **Colic in breast-fed babies due to cow's milk protein:**
Jacobsen, I. and Lindberg, T. (1978). *Lancet*, **2**, 437.
Evans, R. W. et al (1981). *Lancet*, **1**, 1340.
Jenkins, C. H. C. (1981). *Lancet*, **2**, 201.

(93) **Contraception and lactation:**

Gray, R. H. (1975). *International Planned Parenthood Federation Medical Bulletin* (December), **9**, 6.

Baer, E. C. and Winnicott, B. (1981). Special issue on breast feeding: *Studies in Family Planning*, **12**, 123–206.

(95) **Dental caries:**

Robinson, S. and Naylor, S. R. (1963). *British Dental Journal*, **115**, 250.

Stimmler, L. et al (1973). *Archives of Disease in Childhood*, **48**, 217.

(96) **Dental malocclusion:**

Bertrand, F. M. (1968). *Central African Journal of Medicine*, **14**, 226.

Simpson, W. J. and Cheung, D. (1976). *Journal of Canadian Dental Association*, **42**, 124.

(98) **Drugs in breast milk:**

Anderson, P. O. (1979). *Seminars in Perinatology*, **3**, 271–8.

Berlin, C. M. (1981). *Obstetrics and Gynaecology*, **5** (Supplement) 17S.

(105) **Engorgement:**

The Ellis Expressor mentioned here is obtainable from NMAA, PO Box 47, Asquith, New South Wales 2078 Australia.

(113) **Effects of formula feeding in developing nations:**

Berg, A. (1973). *The Nutrition Factor.* Brookings Institute, Washington.

Consumers' Union USA (1975). *Formula for Malnutrition.*

Documents are available from the International Council on Infant Food Industries, Geneva or Baby Milk Action Coalition, Carlton Road, London, for opposing views.

(116) **Formula preparation mistakes:**

Jones, R. A. C. and Belsey, E. M. (1978). *British Medical Journal*, **2**, 211. (Also refers to Table 2, p. 27.)

Martin, J. (1978). *Infant Feeding.* HMSO, London.

Martin, J. and Monk, J. (1982). *Infant Feeding 1980.* Office of Population, Censuses and Surveys. HMSO, London.

(116) **'Drip-milk' collector:**

This is available from Eschman, Oxford.

(119) Iron supplementation of breast-fed babies:

Committee on Nutrition, American Pediatric Association (1976). *Pediatrics*, **58**, 765.

McMillan, J. A. et al (1976). *Pediatrics*, **58**, 686.

Saarinen, U. M. and Siimes, M. A. (1978). *Journal of Pediatrics*, **93**, 177.

Oski, F. A. (1979). *Seminars in Perinatology*, **3**, 381.

Siimes, M. A. (1979). *Acta Pediatrica Scandinavica*, **68**, 29.

(120) Jaundice and breast feeding:

Hargreaves, T. and Piper, R. F. (1971). *Archives of Disease in Childhood*, **46**, 195.

(122) Lactation suppression:
Walker, S. et al (1975). *Lancet*, **2**, 842.

(124) Cow's milk allergies:

Goldman, A. S. (1977). In *Food and Allergy* (edited Hambraeus, L.). Almquist and Witsell, Stockholm.

Jelliffe, D. and Jelliffe, E. P. F. (1978). *Human Milk in the Modern World*. Oxford University Press, Oxford.

Saarinen, U. M. et al (1979). *Lancet*, **2**, 163.

ALLERGIES IN BREAST-FED BABIES:
Jenkins, C. H. C. (1981). *Lancet*, **2**, 260.

(129) Milk intake; hindmilk and foremilk:
Guthrie, H. A. et al (1977). *Journal of Pediatrics*, **90**, 39.
Pollitt, E. et al (1981). *Early Human Development*, **5**, 201.

SELF-REGULATION OF INTAKE:
Ounstead, M. and Sleigh, G. (1975). *Lancet*, **1**, 1393.

(131) Milk production:
SWEDEN
Wallgren, A. (1944). *Acta Paediatrica*, **32**, 778.
Lonnerdal, B. et al (1976). *American Journal of Clinical Nutrition*, **29**, 1127.

(132) Heavy water method of determining:
Coward, W. A. et al (1979). *Lancet*, **2**, 13.

AUSTRALIA
Rattigan, S. et al (1981). *British Journal of Nutrition*, **45**, 243.

THE GAMBIA
Prentice, A. M. et al (1981). *Lancet*, **2**, 886.
Whitehead, R. G. and Paul, A. A. (1981). *Lancet*, **2**, 161.

(134) **Improving milk supply—metoclopramide in:**
Karpilla, A. et al (1981). *Journal of Clinical Endocrinology and Metabolism*, **52**, 436.

OXYTOCIN SPRAY IN:
Ruis, H. et al (1981). *British Medical Journal*, **2**, 340.

(140) **Nipple discharge:**
O'Callaghan, M. A. (1981). *Australia and New Zealand Journal of Obstetrics and Gynaecology*, **21**, 214.

(143) **Nutrition of breast-feeding mothers:**
Aebi, H. and Whitehead, R. (1980). *Maternal Nutrition during Pregnancy and Lactation*. Huber, Bern.

(145) **Feeding of premature babies:**
Gibbs, J. et al (1977). *Early Human Development*, **1**, 227.
Lucas, A. et al (1978). *Early Human Development*, **2**, 251.
Barrie, H. (1982). *Lancet*, **1**, 284.
Davies, D. P. et al (1982). *Lancet*, **1**, 568.

(149) **Re-lactation:**
Avery, J. L. (1973). *Induced Lactation: A Guide for Counselling and Management*. J. J. Avery, Denver, Colorado.
Auerbach, K. G. (1981). *Journal of Tropical Pediatrics*, **27**, 52.

(157) **Solids – what kind?**
Choice (1978). **19**, 187. (This is the Journal of the Australian Consumers' Association.)

(162) **Underfeeding:**
Davies, D. P. (1979). *Lancet*, **1**, 541.
Letter (1979). *Lancet*, **1**, 732.

(169) **Work and breast-feeding mothers:**
Bowlby, J. (1969). *Attachment and Loss*, volume 1: *Attachment*. Basic Books, New York.
van Esterik, P. and Greiner, T. (1981). *Studies in Family Planning*, **4**, 184.

Further reading

(*Recommended in consultation with the Nursing Mothers' Association of Australia.*)

Brewster, Dorothy, *You Can Breast Feed Your Baby ... Even in Special Situations*, Emmaus, Pa, Rodale Press, 1979. 596 pages.
   Covers a very wide range of medical and general 'special' situations for both mother and baby, e.g. diabetic mother, cleft palate baby, re-establishment of breast feeding, hospitalization of mother or baby. Encouraging and supportive.

Goldfarb, Johanna and Tibbetts, Edith, *Breast-feeding Handbook*, Hillside, New Jersey, Enslow Publishers, 1980. 256 pages.
   Written in non-technical terms for health professionals, this book deals with common breast-feeding situations. It is comprehensive and easy to consult.

Haagensen, C. D., *Diseases of the Breast*, 2nd edition, (Chapters 1–3) London, Saunders, 1971.
   This classic textbook on diseases of the breast has three introductory chapters on the anatomy and physiology of the breast.

Haire, Doris and John, *The Nurse's Contribution to Successful Breast Feeding and the Medical Value of Breast Feeding*. Hillside, New Jersey, International Childbirth Education Association Inc, 1974. 68 pages.
   A practical manual for health professionals, especially those working in obstetric hospitals.

Kitzinger, Sheila, *The Experience of Breast Feeding*, Harmondsworth, Middlesex, Penguin Books, 1979. 256 pages.

A practical and supportive book for mothers and fathers. The social, environmental and psychological aspects of breast feeding are especially well covered.

La Leche League International, *The Womanly Art of Breast Feeding.* 3rd edition, Franklin Park: La Leche League International, 1981. 368 pages.
    Written by American La Leche League breast feeding counsellors for mothers. This up-dated edition offers more information than the previous editions, but has the same warm, personal approach. The many photographs are a delight.

Nursing Mothers' Association of Australia, Booklets on breast feeding and mothering from Nursing Mothers' Association of Australia, PO Box 230, Hawthorn, Victoria.
    NMAA publishes a comprehensive range of over twenty booklets which are cheap, simple and deal with specific topics or problems. For example: *Increasing Your Supply*; *And So to Family Foods*; *Breast Feeding After a Caesarean Birth*; *Weaning*; *Inverted Nipples*; *Coping with Breast Refusal*; *Why is My Baby Crying?*

Phillips, Virginia, *Successful Breast Feeding*, 3rd edition, Hawthorn, Nursing Mothers' Association of Australia, 1982. 184 pages.
    A clear, practical and easy-to-read guide for mothers, written with Australian conditions in mind. Virginia Phillips is a Breast-feeding Counsellor for NMAA and the book reflects her wide experience.

Raphael, D, *The Tender Gift – Breast Feeding*. New York, Schoken, 1977.
    This Americo-centric book discusses the doula concept, and digresses into an anthropological and anthropomorphic discussion of breast feeding.

Stables, J., *A Mother's Guide to Breast Feeding*, London, Star Books. 1980.

Stanway, Penny and Andrew, *Breast is Best*, London, Pan Books. 1978. 208 pages.
    The Stanways are both parents and doctors, so their book is

comprehensive. It is a thorough guide to breast feeding and includes detailed technical information on the advantages of breast feeding for those who want more than the basics.

Notes for United States readership

Drugs are rarely prescribed to nursing mothers: readers should consult with their own doctor if there is any doubt in their mind.

The weight of the baby is judged in relation to its height.

Fluoride and iron are usually prescribed routinely.

Equivalent terms

UK	USA
teat	nipple (rubber)
nappy	diaper
dummy	pacifier
oestrogen	estrogen
mei-tai	snuggle
crèche	baby-care center
intragastric tube	gavage
pethidine	meperidine (Demerol)

Equivalent measures

28 millilitres (ml)	= 1 fl oz
570ml	= 1 pint (Imperial)
1000ml (1 litre)	= $1\frac{3}{4}$ pints (Imperial)
28 grams (g)	= 1 oz (ounce)
454g	= 1 lb (pound)(16oz)
1000g (1 kilogram(kg))	= 2 lb 3 oz

Useful organizations

United Kingdom

Association of Breast-Feeding Mothers
131 Mayow Road
London SE2 4HZ

La Leche Great Britain
Box 3424
London WC1 6XX

The National Childbirth Trust
9 Queensborough Terrace
London W2 3TB

Australia

Nursing Mothers' Association of Australia
357 Burwood Road
Hawthorn, Victoria

Childbirth Education Association (Victoria) Ltd
116 Glenferrie Road
Malvern, Victoria

Childbirth and Parenting Association of Victoria
c/o Wyreena Community Centre, Hull Road
Croydon, Victoria

United States of America

International Childbirth Educational Association
PO Box 20048
Minneapolis, MN 55420

La Leche League International Inc
9616 Minneapolis Avenue
Franklin Park, Illinois 60131

Fiji

Mrs C. Weir, USP, SNR
Box 1168
Suva, Fiji

Hong Kong

La Leche League Hong Kong
c/o Mrs D. Robins, Flat 55, 9th Floor
37 Conduit Road, Hong Kong

Kenya

Breastfeeding Information Group
PO Box 59436
Nairobi, Kenya

Malaysia

Persatuan Penasihat Penyusan Ibu Malaysia
3rd Floor, 8 Jalan Klyne
Kuala Lumpur 01–21
Malaysia

Nursing Mothers' Association of Penang
c/o Mrs R. Douglas, 9 Jalan Chenlar
Tanjong Tokong
Penang, Malaysia

New Zealand

La Leche League New Zealand
PO Box 2307
Christchurch, New Zealand

Norway

Ammehjelpen
Postboks 15
Holmen, Oslo 3
Norway

Papua-New Guinea

Susu Mamas, PO Box 5857
Boroko
Port Moresby, Papua-New Guinea

Philippines

c/o Cynthia, Marie Building
F Rodriguez and New York Streets, Cubao
Quezon City, Philippines

Singapore

Singapore Breastfeeding Mothers' Group
CASE Committee, Trade Union House Annexe
Shenton Way, Singapore 0106

Solomon Islands

Lukautim Picanini
c/o Mrs S. Perkins, PO Box 677
Honiara, Solomon Islands

South Africa

Breastfeeding Association
c/o Child Care Information Centre, Rondebosch/Mowbray Hospital
c/o Red Cross Hospital
Rondebosch 7700, South Africa

Vanuatu

Vanuatu Nursing Mothers' Group
c/o Mrs C. Kirkpatrick, PO Box 257
Port Vila, Vanuatu

Index